DATE DUE			

INSTINCT

INSTINCT

The Power
to Unleash
Your Inborn Drive

❖

T. D. Jakes

New York Boston Nashville

FaithWords
Hachette Book Group
237 Park Avenue
New York, NY 10017

www.faithwords.com

Printed in the United States of America

RRD-C

First Edition: May 2014
10 9 8 7 6 5 4

FaithWords is a division of Hachette Book Group, Inc.
The FaithWords name and logo are trademarks of Hachette Book Group, Inc.

The Hachette Speakers Bureau provides a wide range of authors for speaking events. To find out more, go to www.hachettespeakersbureau.com or call (866) 376-6591.

The publisher is not responsible for websites (or their content) that are not owned by the publisher.

Library of Congress Cataloging-in-Publication Data has been applied for.

ISBN 978-1-4555-5404-1 (hardcover)

*I would like to dedicate INSTINCT to the
TDJ Enterprise staff and team who allowed me to
learn to lead while leading them. To the Potter's
House family—your hunger to know drove me to
dig deeper in life. To my many friends who
challenged me, inspired me, prayed for me, and
encouraged me along the way. I always tried to make
sure you knew who you were and your value to me.*

*To my loving wife, Serita, and my five gifted children,
Jamar, Jermaine, Cora, Sarah, and Dexter. To my
siblings, Ernest and Jacqueline. You are all my family,
I love you dearly! I've learned so much from you all
about life and love and what matters most. I'm sure
I couldn't have survived without you giving me a
reason to grow on! Thank you for giving me the
gift of having you in my life!*

Contents

Contents

INSTINCT

CHAPTER 1

⌗

Instinct Has a Rhythm

Our instincts are the treasure map for our soul's satisfaction. Following our instincts can make the crucial distinction between what we are good *at*— our vocation or skill set—and what we are good *for*— the fulfillment of our purposeful potential. When you're truly engaged with your life's calling, whether in the boutique, the banquet hall, or the boardroom, you rely on something that cannot be taught.

I'm convinced that our instincts can provide the combination we need to align our unique variables with our callings and release the treasure within us. When harnessed, refined, and heeded, our instincts can provide the key to unlocking our most productive, most satisfying, most joyful lives.

We often recognize people who seem to thrive by instinct. Fashion designers who do what they do beyond the training they received, with a flair for the latest trends that's inherent and instinctive. Interior decorators and others in the graphic arts may wield this gift as well, but they are not the only ones. Athletes in the "zone," or investors with a keen sense of timing, performers with the courage to audition for a role outside their fans' expectations. They all know what it means to function by their own unique internal compass.

If you have ever had the privilege of working with someone like this, then you know they can take the mundane and make it magical. They can take the most simplistic equipment and produce the most superlative results. Often they maximize their training with their unique flair. No matter what you call it, the truly gifted simply have that extra something that seemingly others don't have or don't tap into the way they should.

Unfortunately, much of what I see today isn't about fulfilling one's true potential as much as it is about appearing to fulfill what other people expect. Too many people want the appearance of winning rather than the practices and hard work that create a true champion. They mistake the prize for the art of winning and will ultimately buy a trophy without ever running a race. They didn't take the class; they bought the diploma. They aren't successful; they just have the props. They aren't driven to achieve something; they just bust their gut to appear busy to everyone around them.

The irony is what these people fail to realize. When you're living by instinct, then you will naturally enhance everything and everyone around you. In other words, success will come naturally! When both your intellect and instincts are aligned, then producing the fruits of your labors brings satisfaction beyond measure.

Now, it will still require hard work and dedication on your part, but the internal satisfaction will fuel your desire to achieve even larger dreams. Based on the fact that we are all inherently creative people, if we are in touch with our instincts, then we will naturally increase our endeavors. When you don't become fixated on winning the prize or appearing successful, and instead pursue your passions, then you will discover the fulfillment that comes from living by instinct.

Feel the Rhythm

Consider this: scientists tell us that even our cells have instincts. Imagine my amazement when I spoke with physicians who revealed the way our physical cells operate. They say even our cells function based on what has been genetically programmed within them. Instinct is interwoven into the very fiber of our DNA.

We all begin as a single cell, a product of an egg and a sperm. They unite to form a zygote, the result of the fertilized egg, the single cell that will evolve from a human *forming* to become a human *being*. This new cell undergoes a series of rapid divisions that produce a blastocyst, the initial ball of new cells. The blastocyst then multiplies into many daughter cells. One expert describes these cells as being "pluri-potential." In other words, each of these cells has the potential to differentiate into new cells of many different varieties. Some "daughter cells" instinctively become skin cells, bone cells, spleen cells, and cardiac cells or brain cells. The inherent imprint of these cells activates them to become what they were predestined to be.

This inherent sense of identity based on function is truly astounding. Doctors explain that the cardiac cells are "auto-rhythmic" cells. They actually vibrate and beat together instinctively at the same tempo—*before* they ever unite with each other and function as the heart! Even drummers in an orchestra need a conductor to set a rhythm, but these cells instinctively catch the same beat and have the same rhythm. They draw together and beat together to the same rhythm.

Learning about these "cell instincts" made me think of the old camp song taken from the Old Testament book of Ezekiel—you know, the foot bone connected to the leg bone and the leg bone connected to the hip bone and so forth. Now, I'm not a doctor, and I'm sure not here to sing around a campfire. But what I want you to see is that the body develops by cells that find their rightful place because they know what they were made to do! These cells vibrate to the tempo of their purpose even before they're operating and performing their function.

So how about you—are you in sync with your inner wisdom about your strengths, abilities, talents, and unique contribution to the world? Or is your life somehow offbeat to your inner melody? Have you lost your rhythm because you have not found your place to define and activate your unique contribution? One of the great tragedies of life is not discovering the people, culture, and careers that are part of your tribe and moving to the same beat.

You may have experienced the discord that comes when those around you move to the beat of a drummer different than your own. Successful businesses, healthy relationships, and most collaborative endeavors require a syncopated alignment of roles, responsibilities, and rhythms. Entrepreneurs often need employees with a work ethic and flexibility similar to their own. It's frustrating when you have an urgent idea that requires execution at midnight and a team member who cannot be reached until the following day. It's not wrong to set boundaries and limits on work, but people need to be on the same page of music so the orchestra can play together. Similarly, romantic partners often discover they're out of step because one desires a waltz while the other's leading a tango.

Contentment comes when you find the people, places, and events in life you were created to impact. Most individuals who lead rich, productive lives do so because they allow their instincts to guide them to the intersection of the head and heart, the place where their deepest passions and sharpest skills align with destiny. They succeed instinctively because they each know their own tempo and recognize it in the individuals and institutions with whom they collaborate.

Connect to Your Calling

If you have ever felt misaligned, this book is for you. If you have lost the rhythm, the passion, or the thrill of living in alignment that you once glimpsed, then keep reading. As he did with the very cells that comprise our bodies and the dry bones that were joined together for new life, God has given us deeper instincts to be attracted to those things that fit a higher and better purpose.

Never settle for less than God's best for your life.

Some people have the courage to move beyond the ordinary, from the methodical mediocre into the revolutionary realization of where they belong. You can have this sense of belonging only when you connect to your core calling. If you believe in calling, as I do, you understand it's more than the motivation to minister that clergy experience. The calling to creativity, the calling to teach, to give, to build, are all part of allowing your instinct to guide you to the "something more" that you suspect is out there.

Who can deny that some people move into their life's purpose with the skill of a child prodigy when he first touches a violin? They're aware of a compelling sense of attraction and engagement that cannot merely be taught but can only be caught. I've known musicians who played the piano from childhood, many without lessons. They just sat down at the keyboard and felt connected to it.

It's a sad thing to live your life without this deep-rooted sense of connection to your purpose. Like a lightbulb without a lamp, this kind of disconnect fosters dark and foreboding feelings in the soul. Whether you are the manager or the employee, the homemaker or the home builder, what matters most is that you have been awakened to your purpose and enlightened to the inner fulfillment that it affords.

Early in my life I myself was haunted by feelings that I was created for more than I could access in my environment. The only reason I moved beyond the many potholes and pit stops I encountered is because of an instinctive allure pulling me toward something up ahead on the road that I had to find! I refused to stop and settle for less than the explosive exploration of what God had placed within me.

There is no secret formula for learning to listen to your instincts. These pages before you merely offer my sparks toward kindling the blaze of your own incandescent, instinctive alignment, the deeper and fuller life you were created to attain. So as we journey together, let's remove the smoke and mirrors and ask the questions at the heart of our truest self. If we seek meaning in our motives, perhaps the answer will not be the voice of God shouting at us from the heavens but in the whisper of our God-given instincts deep within.

You see, Scripture tells us, Out of the heart flow the issues of life (Prov. 4:23). The heart can't read. It can't draw and it surely can't drive. But if we will listen to its drumbeat, if we have the courage to be wooed by its wisdom, then we will find our answer. We could spend the rest of our lives in a rhythm so in sync that the melodious sounds we make transform all areas of our lives into an integrated, harmonic symphony of satisfaction.

As we grow and go forward, our master Creator may be wooing you instinctively into a place where your intellect can flourish and your heart can rest. If cells move until they connect and form the highly complicated and efficient beings we call humans, then maybe we need to put our ears to the heart of the matter and catch the beat. Maybe we need to stop choosing people purely by résumés and rationales that have led us headfirst into disappointment. We need instead to find people who are in sync with our beat and form a more perfect union with those who hear the same rhythm! It is time for us to find the thing we were created to do, the people we were meant to affect, and the power that comes from alignment with purpose.

Having had unique opportunities to sit at the table with champions in almost every imaginable field today, I've found that people who accomplish massive feats don't play by man-made rules. They are trend-setters and game changers. They lead the world into paradigm shifts that we can only study after they've done what they set out to do. They negotiate unprece-dented deals, build beyond borders, and innovate vir-tually every area with amazing accomplishments.

They do it because they don't play out their lives by prewritten scripts. They aren't afraid to leave the cages of comfort and head to the jungles of judicious risk and discovery. These people of whom the world takes notice dare not to fit in but aren't afraid to stand out. They don't run in a pack or stay with the herd. They know where they're going and where they belong.

I'm not suggesting that we take our script from oth-ers. The low-grade plagiarism of popularity will never lead you to true contentment. But I am saying perhaps it is possible to learn from the risk-takers committed to living instinctively, listening beyond information and example, for the inspiration of igniting your pur-pose. If you are already doing what you were created to do, then I want to help you enhance your success. And if you are not, I hope your days of following other drummers will diminish as you listen for the unique, syncopated beat within yourself.

If you listen, it will guide you like a magnet to steel. All else is misguided. Most people are manipulated by the approval of others, the paycheck that supports them, and the lifestyle that has handcuffed them to the brass ring of perceived success. On this path we eventually live like slaves to a man-made system. We chase the goals of others instead of pursuing our own dreams. We anesthetize our despair with the next purchase, pill, or plunder. We do what we think we should instead of living beyond what logic alone can dictate.

If these words resonate with you and reverberate with what you know to be true, then it's time to decode your own instincts, increase your areas of advancement, and illuminate the dark corners of disappointment at the edges of your life. I truly believe that following your instincts will transform your workplace, liberate your career, and enhance your relationships.

Make no mistake, these pages can only offer you clues to stimulate your own process of discovery. The answers you seek are already inside you. So if you're ready to unlock the confines of where you are to discover the freedom of where you were meant to be, then let's get started. *Your* instinct *is the key!*

CHAPTER 2

⋯◇⋯

Basic Instincts

It's the way mother birds build nests, and build them high enough to elude predators. It's the way bees know to extract pollen and return with it to their hive. Or the way that sheep, cattle, and other animals often travel in herds so that they will not be as vulnerable. It's the surge a mother bear experiences to protect her cubs when confronted by a startled hiker in the forest. Biological instinct is the fierce determination of the majestic lion to guard his territory.

These creatures don't have to be taught how to do these things; they are born with the natural instinct to behave in these ways. In fact, most scholars define an instinct as a genetically hardwired tendency, a behavior that's built in and automatic, not learned or conditioned. The survival instinct is generally regarded as the strongest in most every species. Instincts to nurture, to gather, to procreate, to secure food and water, to protect and to defend—these sustain life in practical, very tangible ways.

On a basic level, we share many of the same instincts. We see instinct in action when a baby tries to suckle in order to receive nourishment, or a toddler recoils from a hot skillet. It's the sense you have about the stranger lingering behind you on your walk home that causes you to run into a store and call a taxi. Similarly, no one has to teach you to dodge the oncoming bus careening toward you while you're crossing the street.

We are wired to stay alive. Our bodies naturally seek out nourishment (food and water) and protection (such as shelter, clothing, and weapons) to survive. You've probably heard of the "fight or flight" response, which is an instinctive reaction to any perceived danger. Many scientists also believe that language is instinctive, or at least the desire to express our responses to both internal and external stimuli. Some researchers believe that we are instinctively spiritual beings as well, which of course I would confirm.

Our Instincts Evolve

As we grow and mature into men and women, our various instincts also evolve and become more sophisticated and personalized—but so does our reliance on intellect, evidence, and technology. We are assaulted by so much information each day that it's easy to lose touch with the voice inside us, the compelling sense of knowledge, the awareness we have in our gut.

In addition, we're often conditioned to dismiss our instincts as primal and animalistic, subjective and unscientific. We're taught to rely on facts and figures, data and digits, not hunches and gut feelings. Some people may even consider relying on instinct in the same way they regard superstitions and mental telepathy: fodder for science fiction and superhero movies.

Sometimes we rely on our instincts without even realizing it. We notice details about how a job applicant has dressed and groomed himself and form an accurate opinion about his qualifications. Perhaps we sense the timing is right to have a difficult but necessary conversation with someone in our family and find them receptive when approached. It could be an inexplicable attraction toward one particular field of study or area of business. For instance, you can't help but notice the lines of other people's clothing, wondering about the fabric: how it drapes; its shape, color, and fit. Maybe you've always been fascinated by the way numbers work and enjoy creating order by making the columns balance. Whether you recognize those glimpses of instinct or not, it's there.

On the other hand, our instincts are not necessarily accurate all the time. That hunch about someone else's business deal wasn't true. Your sense of timing for the big date wasn't on target after all. The sense of dread about a client's reaction to your work proved to have no basis in reality. Your intuition about getting the promotion wasn't accurate.

So how do you become more aware of your unique, naturally developed instincts? And perhaps more important, how do you discern when to trust your instincts and when to rely on logic, fact, and objectivity?

Obviously, this is where our relationship with instinct gets tricky.

And that's what this book is all about.

You Just Know

Not one of us is born without instincts. A person is more likely to be born without sight than to be born without insight. In fact, many of my blind friends rely upon insight. All of us have internal senses beyond the physical with which we can better determine what's next, what's safe, or even what's right. Our instincts speak to us daily, prompting us to pay attention, to listen more carefully, to sidestep danger, and to seize an opportunity.

Some may be more in tune with their instincts. And some may be less inclined to listen to them. But we, like all of God's creatures, come complete with them on the inside. From this inner sanctum springs wisdom we don't even know we possess. But in a fast-paced, busy world, we tend not to give ourselves the quiet moments of reflection that are needed to unleash them.

Think about it: there are some things you just *know.* You don't even know how or why you know, you just do. This inner knowing is instinctive. It is as natural as the ability to sense when you've found the thing you were born to do. Unfortunately, many of us often spend our lives doing what we were trained to do. Some do what they were asked to do. And most of us do what others need us to do. And all the while, we wonder why the feeling of fulfillment eludes us.

Our Creator designed everything he made to have a purpose. Yet most of us live our lives wondering what our purpose is. Worse still, there's an aching in our hearts as we sense that there has to be more in life, something beyond the monotonous compliance with convenient opportunities to which most of us have lived our lives. I encounter so many people who dread going to work, not because they are lazy but because they are unfulfilled.

Without understanding the guidance that our innate God-given instincts provide us, we simply adjust to the urgency of circumstances, all the while sensing deep within that we were created for so much more. Yet the uncertainty or fear of pursuing this inner sense keeps us contained in the contrived cage of the ordinary. Simply put, we've never learned to rely on our instincts.

But regardless of where we are in life, it's not too

late to align our lives with the inner wisdom of who we really are and what we were made to do. God, the master designer, has equipped us with a fundamental instinct that draws us to our divine purpose. This sense of potential being realized is more fulfilling than any paycheck. It is the feeling of fitting in, like a piece in a puzzle, to form a greater picture than what we may be doing right now. It is the innate satisfaction that comes from giving the gifts that you and you alone can contribute to the world.

Once we embrace this instinct of identity, we understand why we are so shaped and designed. We realize why we were rejected in other places, why we grew bored by other roles, and why over and over we're haunted by the possibility that there's some place, some plan, some design to which we should be aligned. Deeply spiritual people pray for it to be revealed. Other people wander for the lack of it.

But the most fulfilled, confident people live their lives in the very midst of it. These individuals have answered the question, moved into the sweet spot, and been guided by a God whose design is revealed in them. When we have the courage to leave the familiar and step into the destiny to which our instincts keep drawing us, we can live the same way.

I am not writing a book to show you how to get rich, because I know that many rich people have not identified their purpose. I am not writing to share how to be famous. Too many famous people are miserable.

I write to share with you the importance of being led into your fulfilled purpose by leaving the confines of your conventional cave and entering the space where your heart longs to reside.

The place you will discover when instinct is your guide.

CHAPTER 3

⬡

Instinct in Action

Instincts are the product of what we have and what we want to have. They are the inner compass guiding us from where we are to where we want to go. Perhaps this explains why artists, inventors, and entertainers may be more in tune with their instincts than bankers, engineers, and accountants are with theirs. It's not that these latter professions do not require the power of necessity to stimulate innovation; it's simply that these fact-based fields rely on numbers, equations, and balanced ledgers as their building blocks.

Creative careers, on the other hand, require participants to produce something new from more malleable materials such as words, images, and music. This kind of resourceful resilience often emerges in childhood, requiring some to rely on instinct more than others, not just to survive but also to thrive. This was certainly my experience, the way my own instincts were initially activated.

Being a relatively poor boy born in the hills of West Virginia, I grew up with meager means but with an enormous work ethic instilled by my parents. We lived in a bedroom community in the suburbs of Charleston, and its topography, punctuated with stately trees and rolling hills, abundantly provided one of its more pristine features. However, none of its natural opulence succeeded in camouflaging its economic limitations. Still, it was the matrix that developed me, and now I can more adeptly see why.

Growing up, I was a little chocolate-colored boy with short pants and greased knees tromping through the neighborhood. I'm sure I must have glistened from the Vaseline my mother used to moisturize my skin, but since I had few friends and an overactive energy level, no one seemed to notice. As a result, I spent a great deal of time outdoors, and must confess that since my first name is Thomas I became a bit of a "Peeping Tom."

Yes, I know how that sounds, but I don't mean it to connote someone spying inappropriately who will eventually get arrested! Instead I simply mean that I learned by watching and allowing what I saw to become fuel for my imagination. A voyeur of life and people, I witnessed events and ideologies that became the catalyst for many of my adult conclusions and an impetus of the logic with which I attack life.

You see, research from observation can be quite conclusive. This explains why scientists have laboratories and not just libraries. It is why lawyers seek an eyewitness at a crime scene to testify at a trial. What we see often creates quite an impact. But it's how we process it internally that influences our instincts.

Now, I realize that everyone didn't come from my era or environment. But any time you have been denied a passage to privileges and access to opportunities, you have a tendency to develop a certain adaptation, sensitivity, and instinct through which you compensate for that denial. And it is the development of this instinct for success that is the catalyst of my focus, research, and now writing of this book.

I've climbed high enough in life to peek into the minds of some of the most accomplished people in the world—award-winning entertainers, world-class athletes, and world-changing political leaders. Having come from meager and mediocre beginnings, I am astutely aware of my surroundings when allowed an actual glimpse into the lives of those usually seen only from the distance of blogs and news reports.

Over the years, both through my business and my ministry, I've had dinner with many of them and been entertained in their homes. I have had intense conversations that lasted until the restaurant closed and have observed their families and friends and listened to stories about how they became who they are. I've been on the set of their movies and visited the Oval Office of their leadership, watching them do what they do, discovering what shaped who they are.

I've seen their instincts in action.

Highly Evolved

I've learned that most highly successful people didn't develop in an environment of success; they evolved into it. When obscurity precedes any level of accomplishment, it does so as a mother birthing a child. First generations of successful people are often shocked to find that giving their children all they dreamed of providing doesn't necessarily create the same skills and ambitions in their kids that their own parents' lack of resources instilled in them.

Born in the 1920s, my parents were raised in an industrial age where the primary goal was to get a great job, earn a gold watch, and draw a modest pension when you retire. My mother was a strong advocate for education, and she recommended getting a degree in something marketable so you would always have a job, maybe even a management position of which her generation was enamored. Rightfully so, as their parents were sharecroppers in the Deep South who spent their lives picking peas, sawing lumber, and living off the land.

Now, my parents' ideals are good ones, and I support

them to the highest. But my parents could only promote us to the levels to which they themselves had been exposed. This is why you can't imagine my astonishment when I pulled back the curtain on the Steve Jobses of the world, the Bill Gateses of the world, and others, only to find that some of the most influential leaders of our day either didn't have a degree or didn't have a degree in the area in which they became most well known.

There is no doubt that these men and women are quite intelligent. And through that intelligence, they would without question have reached some modicum of success. But what blew my mind was the discovery that somewhere along the path of intellectualism they either took a detour based on an instinctive decision or incorporated an instinctive move that lifted them completely out of the league of their peers and enabled them to be the icons of power they are today! In other words, these successful icons not only had great instincts, but they were dialed into them and acted on them.

I noticed that most of my new constituents discovered the ideals, products, or passion they have now come to epitomize (and many of them were way past the age of twenty when they did!) by blazing their own trails. These men and women listened to the promptings within them and had the courage to derail the scripted plans of their lives and take the road less traveled by the inner impulse to go further than what their background would've predicted.

They listened when prompted to that nebulous space undefined within the human soul where they house a navigational system—one that virtually all of us have, even if in most of us it's often underutilized. This innate compass provides guidance in answering the age-old questions: Why am I here? What can I do with the life, gifts, and opportunities I have been allotted?

Instincts provide us with information that has been synthesized through the filter of who we really are and our truest goals in life. Facts, data, information, and knowledge provide nourishment and stimulation for this capacity within us. Our powers of observation and of experience are stored here. Our creativity, resilience, and resourcefulness also abide within our instincts. Fused together, the basic instinct in each of us compels us toward the unique fulfillment that is ours alone.

Also, please understand that the kind of instinct we're talking about here is not an uncontrollable urge, self-indulgent desire, arbitrary impulse or compulsion. Instinct may seem similar to these other aspects of our humanity at times, but ultimately our instincts include an acute sense of timing along with an awareness of self and others that transcends selfish lusts and addictive desires. In other words, our instincts are not motivated by immediate gratification, personal gain at the expense of exploitation, or the pursuit of satisfaction untethered from conscience.

Since we are made in the image of our Creator, I'm

convinced that our instincts also bear the imprint of the divine. As human beings, we not only possess the instinct for survival, just as any other living creature does, but we also have instincts for purpose, fulfillment, and dominion. God made us to reflect his creativity, resourcefulness, and imagination. He wants us to see beyond the literal, above the bottom line, and beneath the surface of appearances.

We all have access to the same information and opportunities. But some of us never go beyond what is required to add to the task what is inspired. In this highly competitive world we live in today, meeting the demand will never produce exceptional results. These people exceeded what was commanded of them and veered into the creative to which there was no previous point of reference.

Trailblazing people move by instinct, because there is nothing outward that suggests that what they see inwardly is possible. Like a good detective on a crime scene, they look for clues but don't ignore the unsubstantiated hunches that have often solved cases. They combine instincts with intellect to discover a new way of seeing what's missing in plain sight.

People who combine these two are far more likely to excel than people who only operate according to job descriptions and acceptable past practices. They unlock the undiscovered treasures of instinctively formed creativity; they enhance their life's work by not limiting themselves to the script and structure of other people's minds. As I looked in the window more closely, I noticed that these people did more than shatter glass ceilings—they literally tore the roof off the status quo!

There is indeed a great deal of difference between a job and a career, a place of employment and a rendezvous with destiny. Finding the thing you were created to do can be a dubious task, highlighted by the fact we generally don't have time to do the soul-searching that is required to find the hidden clues to unlock our fullest and best potential. Instead we fill out an application, gain a reasonably good-paying job, and go to work for someone who found the thing they were created to do!

This inward urging or prompting is far too often underutilized, and consequently so many people feel stuck at a certain stage even as they long to be more productive. Beyond pursuing the direction of their instincts, as you may have done at times, the question remains: have you maximized your findings, or only stored the data and acquiesced to the mundane routine of fitting in with what has already been done?

Extra Edge

Now, all of us aren't created to lead a country like the president or compose a classical concerto like Mozart. Instead many of us are, in fact, intended to be a support to these high achievers and realize our dreams by the often-fulfilling task of using our gifts and talents to support a person in power. But even in these roles, the people who live out their opportunities with advancement and promotion do so because they always sense the extra and not just the ordinary!

Whether you work in a government office, a cubicle, a courthouse, or the corner of your apartment, your instincts know truths that can enhance your performance and increase your productivity. There is one thing that is needed to find fulfillment in life: to find that place in life, that station of being, where all that is within you resonates with the challenge before you. This is the spot where inborn natural and innate creativity soars into the horizon of possibility! It's the extra edge that some use and some do not!

Anything that we do for years that doesn't match the inner imprint of our gifting will eventually become monotonous and routine, ritualistic and frustrating. Like a key that will fit a lock and yet is inadequately structured to let us open the door, we find ourselves jammed into a role that fulfills the needs of those around us but may not unlock the door to the larger life, work, and cravings of our inner soul.

If we are to find alignment between the external career and internal call, we are going to have to navigate through the maze of low-hanging opportunities offered to sustain us and fulfill the open-door area of need that awaits us! It is the vision of what is beyond the routine that heightens the blood and stirs the adrenaline within each of us.

There is a satiety achieved when we get out of bed knowing that although the day ahead may be demanding, it can't require something of us that isn't represented within the inventory of what we can handle. In fact, it is often the more challenging job, ministry, marriage that either causes us to shrink away and grumble or activate the creative instinct to find a remedy or create a solution.

This is the choice we face each day.

In a staff development training session with my team recently, I explained to them that at a management level I needed around me people who bring innovative solutions, not people who gain access to my office merely to reiterate problems. Truly great leadership is solution oriented. While it is true that the proverbial buck stops with me, many issues made it to me that should've been resolved before they ever got to me. I further explained that if they weren't participating in the solution, they were by default adding to the problem!

Great instincts lead to great promotion. Since leadership instincts have the power to influence net worth, it may be worth your time to spend a little time enhancing those instincts and acting on them when given the freedom to do so. Because at the end of the day, all that matters in this brief vacation we take on earth is that we didn't shrink into a corner and waste the days we're given doing what we have to do rather than rising and taking on the challenge of becoming all we were created to be.

In order to do this, we must not live in the practical nor the pragmatic but must have the courage to move into the premier. That satisfaction of being able to meet the demands of our lives is in part reached when we have a keen sense of the inner instincts we have of being the right person in the right place at the right time to handle the task. Often the complexity of our lives spawns the creativity in our lives! Our instincts can cut through the clutter of chaos and forge a clear path for us to follow—that is, if we're listening and courageous enough to follow.

But obviously, listening and following is easier said than done.

Instinct from Adversity

When I was a child there were not many gadgets to assist us. Even our toys had few features. Girls had to imagine their hard-bodied Mattel baby dolls were wet and needed changing; we boys had to turn apple trees into army tanks with only our imaginations to guide us. As we played in the backyard while our mothers peeked occasionally out the window, we became quite proficient at turning sticks into baseball bats and rocks into softballs. Left to our own devices, ants transformed into armies and snowflakes evolved into snowmen.

We were forced to be instinctive enough to sense danger when a snake was near or to discern a buddy from a bully while walking home from school! We didn't have to do character assessment from a laptop of who our friends were or search Facebook for common "likes." We didn't realize it then, but those simple circumstances were in fact the gymnasium that gave our instincts a workout. My backyard turned into a jungle. Our little playground toys had all the thrills of a Disneyland designed and created by a child who some would have said had an overactive imagination.

As I look back on those days, it was the necessity of not having enough that spawned the creativity to see the invisible, but I learned how to play in what I dreamed and not in what I had. Today I am most grateful for the clarity of thought and the nimbleness of mind to spark creativity, even though it originated in what sounds like adversity today. Imagination was a coping mechanism through which we were allowed— no, encouraged—to see an inanimate object not just for what it was but what it could be. This ability to see the invisible was a great stimulus for instinctive reasoning.

Maternal Instinct

As poor children we were inspired through the absence of the obvious to tap into the presence of the imagined. I remain grateful to this day that I was given that back-yard wilderness to teach me to dream of what could be without getting lost in what is. Little did I know that, standing in creek water surrounded by scamper-ing rabbits and hawks gingerly perched on branches, I would playfully start a cycle of innovation that would one day be the mother of my own creative instinct!

This is not how we usually define the term *maternal instinct*, but I think it applies just the same. Later as a young pastor I used this same sheer instinct to step into a condemned building and look beyond the deplorable stench and dilapidated walls of its present condition and see what it could be if given some remodeling, care, and enhancement. My instinct became the impe-tus for a vision, for the power of imagining its filled potential, and for the tactical steps needed to create a plan of fulfillment.

As I got older, the same instinct that remodeled the building later became the impetus through which I could salvage a flailing company, or enhance a weak script into a blockbuster movie. Instinct and imagina-tion become the parents of our creative visions. They allow us to see opportunities where others see only limitations. Instead of focusing on what we don't have, we concentrate on what we do have—and what can be created from those ingredients. *People with great instincts always transform what they are given to more than what it was when presented to them!*

The best thinkers, builders, draftsmen, architects, designers, hairstylists, preachers, and chefs are those who walk amongst us with one foot in reality and the other planted firmly in the realm of the potential. If, like them, you're blessed to recognize the gap between where you are and where you want to be, then you may also know that in order to cross over into a more successful, fully realized life, you must allow your instincts to become your bridge.

Our instincts teach us how to take less and do more. Like a gourmet chef with a limited pantry, we combine the various flavors to create something new and delicious. Our instincts up the ante and propel us to the next level. Our instincts illuminate our path amid the bleakness of realities, statistics, and studies and guide us from the mundane to the magical.

Innovators live by their instincts to break barriers and resist complacency. Consider someone like Oprah Winfrey, whose unprecedented business model changed daytime television, not only in terms of content but also even more important, in terms of an innovative business model. Or Cathy Hughes, who changed the game of radio forever by developing models that not only built a communications empire but affected how R&B music would be marketed within our community. Instinctive pioneers such as the Bronner Brothers or the makers of Dudley products, who had the foresight to pioneer hair-care companies that revolutionized how black people purchased beauty products.

When we look at these individuals, it's not enough to simply applaud their success. We must examine their creative propensity through which they created something unique then successfully marketed the fruits of their labors. In other words, it's not enough to know what people did if you can't learn why they did it like they did it. John Maxwell says that those who know how to do a thing will always have a job. But those who understand why they did it will always be their bosses!

The real catalyst of creative instincts is about peeking into the windows of your own heart and soul. Others can inspire you, but ultimately the only thing that empowers you is what lies within you and learning how to better utilize what you've been given.

Even if what you've been given seems wrapped in nothing but problems, these barriers can become breakthroughs. They are just blessings camouflaged as burdens, creek beds from which you will develop oceans, backyard trips that will eventually open your mind to safaris. Whether you are wrestling with a poor marriage, a pathetic career, or a plummeting business, there isn't any area of your life that will not be transformed by your instincts if you're willing to look within and exercise them. If you go beyond the facts and failures, and explore the feelings and impulses you have to increase what you've been given, you will light a trailblazing torch that will illuminate your steps, spark your dreams, and nourish your aspirations.

Isn't it about time you activated what you've been given inside you?

CHAPTER 4

✦

The Elephant Is Ova Dere!

My own life-changing encounter with the power of instinct in action occurred recently, on a safari in South Africa. Yes, the kid who grew up playing in creek beds behind his house now felt an even keener thrill as I found myself lurching over open terrain in a Jeep! In fact, there was no way I could ever have imagined what a truly life-transforming event this safari would become, catapulting me into the "aha! moment" that inspired this book. I wasn't there to stalk big game but to hunt for insight into this new world of roaring lions, zealous zebras, and the creatures that have always, for some unknown reason, fascinated me—elephants!

Air Traffic Control

I had been invited to Johannesburg by a group of black billionaires to discuss faith and finances and how one affects the other. These men and women were among the first to have risen to such heights economically after the Apartheid. It was a very powerful exchange of ideas. We had ended the sessions, and my wife and I had been awarded a complimentary couple of days to recuperate from jet lag and the completion of a grueling schedule marked by several teaching sessions. My host explained that we would have to take a small propeller plane from the city into a more rural location.

Our youngest son, Dexter, was also traveling with us, and he shared an excitement about our excursion that my wife did not. Hours later when I looked down at the narrow patch of pavement doubling as a runway, I understood her trepidation. I looked out the window and couldn't help but notice that there was no control tower, nor anything resembling a terminal.

The place was void of a fixed-base operator or even a house for guests to rest or wait. The lonely little strip used for landing and taking off also had another occupant—a huge rhinoceros was parked in the middle of it and watched us with an implacable expression. Talk about air traffic control!

As we circled around him, hoping he would move and allow us room to land, my wife suggested that we return to the city. However, there was no way the men of our house would be denied this extraordinary adventure of a safari. So we waited patiently until the rhino cleared us for landing and were then transported to a beautiful mansion surrounded by dense trees and small wildlife.

As we unpacked our carry-on bags and got settled, our host warned us not to wander outside the palatial fence surrounding the estate. He warned us that this was not like a visit to the zoo in Dallas, where the animals were caged and the people were free. Instead, we were contained in the house so that the elephants and rhinoceroses would have the liberty to browse the plains without restrictions. As I anticipated the thrilling journey that awaited us the next morning, I felt like Tarzan about to burst with one of his famous yells.

The next morning I was up before the sun and enjoyed a delicious pancake breakfast on the lanai before donning my newly acquired khaki safari suit. We climbed into the Jeep, my son still sleepy but excited about our first day in the bush. Then I met our guide. He was a distinguished gentleman who was incredibly knowledgeable, and I listened intently as he unloaded priceless information about the habitat, the eating and mating habits, and so much more concerning the beasts that inhabited the wild.

Honestly, it all felt a little surreal. Considering my background, I marveled at this "if my mother could see me now" moment. Without a doubt, we were entering a world that couldn't be further from where I grew up. The African wilderness has unspoken rules and regimens that the zoologist guide shared with us as I oriented myself into this new environment so foreign to my background and previous points of reference. There were no street signs, traffic lights, or road manuals, just the voice of the zoologist guiding us along the way.

We saw gazelles leaping in the air like grease spattering in a cast-iron skillet at a fish fry. They skipped and lunged forward so fast that my camera palpitated in cardiac arrest while I snapped away as fast as I could. We spied on lions with their cubs, resting in the shade. Later we watched zebras move like painted horses loosed from a carousel. So much beauty, energy, and primal instinct came alive before us, more vivid and startling than any IMAX, HD, or 3D film could ever hope to capture.

As the sun hovered above the horizon like a scarlet ember, we looked for a place to make camp. It had been a good day, an unforgettable day. My only disappointment, which I kept to myself, was that we had not seen any elephants. The powerful pachyderm had eluded us all day, and as the sunset melted into twilight, I assumed that we had missed our chance. But then our zoologist guide casually mentioned that he looked forward to showing us the elephants tonight.

Had I heard him right? He planned to be out here at night! And for us to be with him? I swallowed hard and acted brave as we persevered deeper and deeper into the entrails of a world completely new and now even more foreboding draped in shadows. Now, there were certainly a lot of animals I did not want to encounter in the dark of the African wilderness. And elephants remained high on that list. Nonetheless, as we continued bouncing along the dimly lit path that was our road, it was clear that our guide intended on saving the biggest, if not the baddest and best, for last.

Soon our driver stopped the Jeep, and a man draped in loose, native garb seemed to appear out of nowhere alongside us. Our guide told us that he was a Zulu, and he would be assisting us this evening. I couldn't help but remember my history classes from junior high about Shaka Zulu the warrior, and I imagined that he might have looked like this stoic, dark-skinned man who proceeded to perch on the edge of our Jeep in a makeshift chair that looked as though it had been welded onto the hood to accommodate his small but muscular frame.

Apparently, he knew where to find the elephants. But based on his silent, impassive demeanor, I wasn't so sure. We hadn't seen one all day. If our zealous zoologist couldn't locate them, how was our new addition going to find them?

Water for Elephants

As our journey continued, the zoologist began spouting a fountain of scientific information about the area.

However, I noticed the Zulu seemed unimpressed by the intellectual prowess of the other man, who continued to lecture with impressive factual data about our surroundings. But the ancient-looking warrior remained silent as we careened deeper into the bush, jostled by bump after bump, until suddenly he opened his mouth and proclaimed, "The elephant is ova dere!"

Seated between a zoologist and a Zulu, between intellect and instinct, I saw something more startling than I had seen all day. I realized that intellect can explain an elephant, but only instinct can find one! The zoologist had used hundreds if not thousands of words to describe the environment where we might find elephants, along with their eating habits, mating patterns, and fighting skills. And yet, the Zulu waited quietly, listening to something even more powerful than his counterpart's knowledge, and uttered five simple words: "The elephant is ova dere!"

Moments later, his instinctive exhortation proved true. Based on the direction the Zulu was pointing in, our driver careened over rocky roads into a clearing by a small lake. There, a herd of elephants lounged and frolicked like guests beside the pool at the Ritz. Throwing water over their heads with their long trunks, they ignored their new spectators and continued cavorting.

I was speechless. Such power and might. Such enormous grace and agility on such a gigantic scale. We took picture after picture and had an incredible time, but I couldn't get out of my mind that God had brought me all the way to South Africa to show me something. Through this simple encounter, he revealed a profound metaphor on how to position my life and career for the future.

You see, it was there that I realized that I must not only surround myself with talented, well-informed people in order to prepare for the future. I must also include those individuals gifted with what the Zulu had afforded us. He reminded me that most things are not captured or conveyed by intellect alone. In fact, intellect without instinct can only explain and explicate but not execute. Only instinct can successfully find what intellect explains.

This is the one thing that university degrees and on-the-job experience cannot instill in you. Your professors and bosses can invest countless hours exposing you to critical information and inspire you with historical empirical data that will be invaluable as you trek through life. But the gift they cannot give you is the instinct to know when to do what only you can do and where to do it!

In order to harness your intentions with your actions, you must rely on instincts. Every visionary learns that they must be well-informed and well-equipped to accomplish their targeted achievements. But they must also be in touch with their instincts in order to use their experience, education, and equipment to fulfill their expectations. Instincts can help connect the dots between where you're trying to go and how you will get there.

Intellect can make a salesman knowledgeable about his product, but it cannot tell him how to read his client. The police academy can teach an officer about crime scenes, but it cannot teach him how to search his gut and go with his instincts. The dating service can bring the right age, IQ, and physical attributes of a possible spouse before you from its extensive database. But it can never accurately measure the actual chemistry that will exist between you and your prospective mate when you finally meet.

The Guide Inside

The lessons of South Africa stayed with me.

I realized that my father certainly knew this truth as he built his one-mop-one-bucket janitorial business into a fifty-two-employee company. Dad had instincts to increase. Great preachers experience this urge as they unload a biblical text. Gifted leaders recognize that knowledge and talent are not enough as they navigate through crucial decisions. Movie stars know the secret to being more than just an actor. Instincts separate the mighty from the mediocre!

How about you? Do you have the instincts to know when you are on to something or when you are just going for a ride? Do you trust your instincts when making a business deal or hiring a new employee? If not, you may attain a modicum of success, but you will never fulfill your maximum potential until you advance from being a zoologist to a Zulu!

This insight changed my prayer life, altered my interview process, revised the way I evaluated effective friendships, and ultimately thrust my vision forward from the ordinary to the extraordinary. All of my life I had thought that some people had it and some people didn't. But I didn't really have a word to describe what my eyes had witnessed. Now I can tell you what "it" was, that crucial difference that makes magic out of the mundane.

Thanks to an encounter at the tip of a continent thousands of miles from my home, I now had a term for the nebulous criteria of successful living. It wasn't just talent. It wasn't just intellect.

I had found the secret of champions. As I went back through all the people I had met in my life like a reel-to-reel tape stuck on rewind, suddenly it all made sense. From concert stages to corporate lunches, from church revivals to courtroom closing statements, the one thing each encounter had in common—instincts!

So if you are going after the big game of an idea, remember elephant tracking requires instincts you may not have had to use chasing rabbit ideas! It isn't just intellect or even understanding. It isn't just gift-edness and opportunity. It is the gift of activated instincts. Where do they come from? How can we sharpen them? How can we utilize what our creative Creator has invested in our deepest parts? Yes, I said "in"-vested in all of us—to adapt, to transform, to create, and to sense moments of significance or danger. Moments to be wary and moments to be warring. When to cringe and when to capture. How to craft and not to crash.

It is the law of instincts that determines how we manage the moment, move into position and adapt, resourcefully create, and strategically forge ahead without fear. The common denominator of instincts wins presidential elections, makes comedians successful, causes architects to build timeless monuments, and elevates engineers to artists.

Living by instinct elevates your ability to know where you're going and how to get there. It can help you know when to slow down and step back and when to accelerate and step up. And it can guide you to what you're ultimately looking for—whether that's the elephant in the room or the elephant ova dere!

CHAPTER 5

⬥

Instinct or Extinct

In order to activate our instincts, I'm convinced everything starts with *exposure*. You cannot be what you do not see. It isn't that exposure gives us instincts; it's that exposure awakens instincts and stops us from ignoring what we know to be true within us. Most people adapt to their environment more quickly than they should. They adjust themselves to the situation rather than adjusting their situation to the dreams they have inside.

You'd be surprised to find that you have accepted and adapted to being much less than what you're capable of becoming. It's alarming that people seek to fit in without considering the power they have to cultivate the gifts they've been given. You may even be mystified as to why you aren't further along in life. You have checked off all the boxes on the recipe for success and yet find yourself falling short. Isn't it time for you to understand what you've been given and how to sift the stirrings within so that your survival instincts can surface?

As the Zulu taught me, you must combine all your ingredients with the inner wisdom that God has given you if you expect to thrive. My prayer is that you will experience the same kind of revelation that struck me while sitting in a Jeep in South Africa as a wizened tribesman proclaimed, "The elephant is ova dere!"

Several years ago when I came to Dallas, I decided I wanted to buy some land and build affordable housing as a way of giving back to my community. I thought it would help many people who couldn't afford a home to be able to bring the cost down to their individual means. My goal was well intended and came from a good heart, but when I begin to gather statistics on the process, I learned something that would inform my hypothesis: people adapt to their own expectations. In other words, we often behave based on our perceptions more than the reality of our actual circumstances.

You see, in this case the reality became clear: people who move into low-cost neighborhoods soon lose interest in repairs and home improvements. If their required investment is small, so is their commitment. They acquiesce to the environment and so do their children. They assume *low-cost* means "inferior quality," "temporary," and "inadequate," which of course is not the case. But it becomes a self-fulfilling prophecy when they neglect their new homes, ignore needed maintenance, and disrespect their opportunity for advancement.

Instead I learned that the wiser way to influence and effect change was to avoid the subtle segregation that creates sociological constructs for the possibility of ghettos. We learned that mixed-income housing creates a stronger tax base, which in turn improves public school systems without subsidies. The result is a win-win: neighbors influence one another in not just community maintenance but through the exchange of ideas that help to raise the diversity in that community!

Often we don't recognize the urgings within us because we haven't been exposed to people who affirmed their importance. If we don't learn to listen to instinct, then we will soon find ourselves extinct! To ignite your own unique instincts, you must recognize how you have handled them thus far in your life. If we are to institute change, then we must recognize the environmental influences to which we've been exposed. Is your perception of reality skewed by what you expect or by what you really desire? Obviously, our attitude and outlook on life have an enormous influence on both the accuracy of our instincts as well as our inclination to be aware of them and trust their guidance.

Instinct of Identity

I have a set of twin boys—well, I say "boys," but my sons are actually grown men now. And while they are fraternal, not identical, twins with the same mother and father, they couldn't be any more different. When they were still in the crib, I noticed each had a distinct personality that continued to evolve and solidify as they developed. One is personable and artsy; the other is quiet and independent. One is nurturing and compassionate; the other is responsible and diligent. One is spontaneous and social; the other is methodical and private.

I'm certainly not a licensed clinical psychologist trained in early childhood development. I'm just a father who started out peeking over their cribs. While my wife and I never intentionally tried to make them conform to the same personality type, I'm sure we assumed that they were more similar in temperament than they actually were. We probably dressed them alike when they were too young to protest and worked to make sure each got equal attention. But clearly they were not alike!

And as they grew through puberty into young adulthood, I continued to ponder how two people so closely intertwined in such a small place as the womb, raised in the same house, and parented in identical environments could gravitate to such different clothing, diverse types of friends, and separate courses of life.

In observing them as adult men, I remain fascinated to watch each of them unpack their inventory of uniqueness and become acquainted with the substance of their individuality as they pursue the fulfillment of their divine potential. It's been an often-raucous adventure as they've explored and discovered their own uniqueness, for each brings a distinctly remarkable thought pattern and skill set to problem solving.

Perhaps the primary reason for their successful development as independent, distinct individuals is their commitment to discover the power of their own unique talents, abilities, and proclivities. They clearly are not clones of each other, and they haven't simply become the opposite reaction of each other.

Because they're twins, though, they probably faced the challenge of self-discovery sooner and more deliberately than most of us. And yet their accelerated journey is the same one we're all traversing: to know who we are created to be, to know why we're here on this earth, and to live out the pursuit of our divine destiny.

Like my twins, many of us share the same variables for success as others around us, and yet we each fail to discover our distinct, personalized combination to unlock that success. Have you ever wondered why people with less talent, fewer resources, and more obstacles than you pass you by? Have you ever attempted to

follow a formula or check off five "easy steps" to fulfillment only to become frustrated and feel like you're the
exception? Too often, we imitate others and conform
to popular standards but fail to tap into our most powerful, most precious resource—*our own uniqueness.*

Obviously, my twin sons shared numerous similarities,
both genetic factors and environmental influences. But
the fact remained that each of them had been divinely
designed as a one-of-a-kind, inimitable reflection of his
Creator—not of his twin or even his parents.

As they matured, my twin sons naturally noticed
the ways in which they differed from each other—
but more important, they relished, cultivated, and celebrated these differences. As I mentioned before, they
were more self-aware and more determined at an earlier age to discover their own unique abilities, interests, and personal passions. As much as they loved
each other and enjoyed being twins, nonetheless they
didn't want to be a duplicate of someone else, certainly
not each other. Like each one of us, each wanted to
know the fingerprint of his own personality.

They were blessed to have both the motivation and
the freedom to explore their inner resources. Growing up, many of us aren't encouraged to identify our
individuality; in fact, we were likely told in both word
and by example to conform, to fit in, to not stand out.
Whether it was overtly expressed or covertly implied,

the message we got was to accept the status quo and not make waves. This may have been our parents' attempt to make life run smoother or even to protect us from the scrutiny, and often cruel mockery, that comes from standing out in a crowd.

And yet, most of us knew at an early age that we were not like everyone else, let alone who others wanted us to be. It might have been our desire to stay indoors and get lost in the adventures of the Hardy Boys or Harry Potter instead of playing pickup basketball in the park. From my experience and observations, our true identity rarely enjoys the freedom to emerge without first enduring conformity, social modification, or outright suppression. Peer pressure as well as parental expectations and the demands of our circumstances all exert various amounts of force on who we really are. Our instincts may have even guided us to hide parts of ourselves in order to keep them alive when we were younger. We instinctively knew that we could not express our creativity, unleash our imagination, or announce our dreams without them being injured by the ridicule, rejection, or retaliation of others.

As adults, however, we now have the power to liberate ourselves. We need no one else's permission to empower the God-given essence of our identity! Whether we think we have the time, money, or other resources needed to uncover who we really are, it's vitally important that we discover our core and allow it to grow, develop, and flourish.

You see, it's not about whether you can afford therapy or complete your education or attend that self-improvement seminar. And it's not about becoming self-absorbed, babying your inner child, or excusing self-indulgence. It's simply about whether you have the courage to look within yourself and embrace all that you find there!

Exposure and Independence

People successfully living by instinct, the innovators, trailblazers, and playmakers, are liberated by their own instinctive drive, the fuel for their own unique GPS systems.

This motivational contrast can inspire, equip, and model for you the areas of development required for progress on your own journey. This helps explain why the mixed-income housing solution mentioned earlier emerged as the most solid, change-inducing one available. We often learn from our differences more than our similarities, and those ascending the ladder of success can watch and learn from those a few rungs above them.

On the other hand, we cannot allow imitation or even emulation to dictate our decisions. Our exposure to others must become fuel and not the engine itself, empowering our self-discovery and energizing our instincts. Perhaps considering the way an artist or a designer works may illuminate the process for us. An artist has natural talent but nonetheless needs instruction, inspiration, and integration in order to produce their own unique innovation.

Their natural talent will get them only so far without input from teachers, peers, and practitioners. An artist's exposure to the great historical works provides a solid foundation that allows the artist to branch out into new areas of experimentation and hybridization. As one writer once told me, "You have to know the rules and the reasons behind them before you can break them!"

I'm convinced awakening our instincts as a guiding force in our lives operates from a similar paradigm. We need to glimpse what has gone before in order to envision the portals of possibility. We must taste the nectar of past necessity if we are to ferment our own nectar for the future! We should take in as much of the view as possible from higher elevations in order for us to acclimate and climb to our own higher summits.

Ultimately, this will require you to step out on your own more than follow in the footsteps of others. The higher you ascend on your own unique path, the fewer the number of trailblazers ahead of you. Allowing your instincts to guide you will be lonely at times. Others, especially those committed to conformity and comfortable in their own cages, may feel threatened as you venture out on your own. They may criticize your passionate pursuits and seek to sabotage your date with destiny.

However, if you live instinctively, these critics will never impede your progress for more than a few moments. In my own life, I've never had a hater who's doing better than me!

The people ahead of you, living in the liberty of instinct-guided uniqueness, will welcome you, encourage you, and mentor you. They will inspire you to be a pioneer and not a poser. Only those incarcerated by their unwillingness to listen to their instincts and to take the risks required for success will seek to deter you.

We'll discuss more about the temporary obstacles these critics might present in an upcoming chapter. But for now, simply realize that both exposure and independence are required if you are to get in touch with your instinctive wisdom and allow it to guide you to the next level of intentional living. Don't allow those less motivated, or committed to tearing down others in an attempt to prop up themselves, prevent you from being all that you can be in the fullness of your special, unique, one-of-a-kind identity.

Decode Your Design

Once you're ready to activate your instinct for success, you must actively seek elements of excellence that inspire you. Are you aware of what truly fascinates you? What appeals to your heart and ignites something deep inside you? The news articles that arrest your attention, the topics that tantalize your thought process, the curiosity that compels your unquenchable questions? These are the areas where you can begin to energize your instincts of identity.

The decoding process does not require a battery of aptitude tests, personality panels, or psychoanalysis. It simply requires you to become a student of yourself. Right now, go and see what you have bookmarked as "favorites" on your computer. Look at the images you've collected on Pinterest—what do they all have in common? Whose Twitter feeds have you been compelled to save and return to again and again? What magazines do you always pick up while waiting in the dentist's office? Which blogs magnetically pull you back to ponder another's observations and affinities?

Please keep in mind, you must be honest with yourself here. Cut through the books on your bedside table that you're *supposed* to read or the Snapchat exchanges you feel *obligated* to return. Others may not know about these interests and excursions in your life, but you know they are there. Your dream to run a bed-and-breakfast. Your curiosity about how to create a new investment portfolio. Your guilty pleasure of reading romance novels. Your ability to sew a jacket that looks like something off the rack.

These are the clues that are all around you, my friend! Use your instincts to guide you to what you love but may not have allowed yourself to admit. Dredge up your favorite memories of childhood and what gave you pleasure. Was it building new, never-before-seen structures with Legos? Creating stories about your friends set on another planet? Caring for your pets with the love and attention of a new parent? Whatever once had the power to float your boat can still rock your world!

It may feel silly or childish at first, embarrassing to admit, or crazy to consider. But search through the archeology of your own ambition. Don't disregard any attraction, interest, passion, or proclivity as being too "out there" to examine and extract information from. You never know what you might discover by thinking outside the box that culture, conformity, and critics have tried to impose.

Once you have a decent list of these personal preferences and uniquely special variables, look for patterns, similarities, and common denominators. Group them according to how they move you, speak to you, motivate you, and stimulate you. What sparks your creative impulse? Who motivates you as a role model? Where do you feel most alive?

Nothing is off-limits as you explore. You are the most fascinating person you will ever know! So don't cover up, deny, suppress, or pretend otherwise. Allow the true you to come out, the softer side, the edgier side, the creative side, the more organized side, the driven side, the liberated side, the "who cares what people think" side, and the "this makes me feel alive" side. This is the soil where you will discover seeds planted long ago waiting to burst through the surface of your consciousness and bear fruit. This is the galaxy of stars that can illuminate your journey through whatever darkness you may encounter. This is the area that can give you the satisfaction of knowing that you and you alone are doing what only you can do.

If this excavation process intrigues you, then I invite you to spend some time uncovering your greatest vital resources. I merely provide these questions and suggestions here as catalysts for this lifelong learning process.

CHAPTER 6

⊏◊⊐

An Instinctive Sense of Direction

Many people seem astounded that I have a finger in so many pies besides ministry—business, writing, speaking, music, film, and television, to name a few—and often inquire about my motivation in exploring such diverse endeavors. They don't realize that my entrepreneurial spirit has always been a part of who I am and where I came from.

Growing up, I watched my father start with a mop and bucket and begin a janitorial service that eventually serviced dozens of schools, offices, and churches. In addition to keeping our house clean and cooking meals, my mother taught school and often worked other jobs to make ends meet. My parents were hardworking people with a unique blend of business savvy, dedication, personal dignity, and financial wisdom, and having them as role models has proved to be an invaluable legacy.

So even after I felt God's call and entered the ministry, I always worked other jobs to pay the bills. Whether it was managing the paint department at Sears, selling men's clothing, or working the assembly line at Union Carbide, I appreciated the value of working hard in order to provide for my family as well as to underwrite my ministry. "Tent-making," as we call it in the church, came naturally to me.

However, when I was laid off at the plant during a time of economic devastation in West Virginia, I faced a new challenge. No one was hiring. No jobs to be had. No employment opportunities within a fifty-mile radius. Becoming a full-time pastor was not an option. My ministry was still in embryonic form and unable to provide compensation; most of the time, I funded the electric bill and meager supplies for the church.

So after looking outwardly for a job, I then looked inwardly for inspiration about how to feed my family and keep us afloat. I learned that if necessity is indeed the mother of invention, then desperation is the father! I didn't have time to ponder which career direction might be the most strategic or to contemplate the business model for a new start-up. Instead I simply relied on my default setting and considered the resources at hand, which wasn't much, and concluded that I could start a lawn mowing service to get us by for a while. With a beat-up old truck, a few secondhand mowers, and a couple of college kids to help me, I was in business.

My little lawn-care company never grew much or exploded into an empire, which doesn't surprise me, because I never had any real passion for it. But it did provide a survival tool for a season, for which my family and I were most grateful. This season also taught me new lessons about myself and my instinct for survival. As tempting as it was to feel angry for being laid off or to feel like a victim of the anemic economy, I was forced to remember that I had choices and responsibilities. It wasn't just my own well-being at stake, but my family's. No one was going to go hungry on my watch!

Whether you're running a tech business or a bakery, a hotel chain or your own household, you must filter adversity through your instinct to survive. When expectations don't run according to plan, you must be willing to change course, adapt your vision, and recalculate what's needed to survive. Every obstacle contains an opportunity. It may not be the doorway to success you were looking for—it may be a second-story window left open just a crack!

Your instincts naturally create a way forward out of whatever you have at hand. Hardship can humble you, but it cannot break you unless you let it. Your instinct for survival will see you through if you're attuned to its frequency. Instinct will find a temporary stopgap without ever taking its sights off your larger goals. There's no greater way to hone your instincts than to overcome adversity. Successful leaders know that instincts transform adversity into opportunity.

Driving the Jeep

As you venture into new jungles of opportunity, the people riding with you make a huge difference in your ability to move forward over rough terrain. While on my safari in South Africa, I appreciated the rugged power and sturdy frame of our carrier vehicle, a Jeep clearly designed for off-road excursions. It adapted to the muddy roads and rocky hills without slowing down. Clearly, it was built for survival under stress.

In order to survive, we must be as rugged and determined as this Jeep navigating through the jungle. We must be willing to make hard choices and accept temporary solutions. And we must also be willing to mobilize those around us to head in the same direction as our destiny. No matter how resourceful, creative, or industrious we may be, without others on our team, we will only idle on our ideas instead of gaining traction toward interaction!

If instinct is the fuel that powers your Jeep, then your team members are the tires!

I don't care how polished the Jeep is or how much horsepower it has under the hood. It may be built for rugged hills and designed to take you on the safari of a lifetime, but if the tires aren't filled up with air and ready to roll, the carburetor, spark plugs, or steering wheel cannot help you move in the direction you need to go.

As we delve deeper into this subject, my supposition is that you want to maximize your journey and enhance your productivity. If all you want is the showroom floor, then wax away. But if you want to be mobile, malleable, and magnificent, then we have to get those who support the vision moving in a synchronized, unrestricted way.

So much of the journey, especially your speed and direction, depend on how you drive and the choices you make about your vehicle. This connection to your instinctive rhythm affects every area of your life, including how you interact with and lead others. I know that when I have my hands on the wheel, the buck stops with me. But the question arises: Which "me" is driving? Am I driving with personality or purpose? Am I driving with my heart or my head? I have often struggled inwardly to understand which part of me leads the way.

We'll explore instinctive leadership styles in chapter 14, but for now, remember instinct requires self-awareness and risk taking. You have to know your areas of gifting and expertise while also not becoming too comfortable. A gifted athlete, performer, or executive will always stretch and extend beyond their present capabilities, using what they've already accomplished as a launching pad.

Never Settle for Status Quo

Routine is the enemy of instinct. So break the mold! While it's important to establish routines, schedules, and systems of operation, it's just as important to know when to change them. Routines without ongoing assessment lead to stagnation and mediocrity. Most individuals, teams, and organizations rise to a challenge or fall to the familiar. It's better to change and fail than to settle for the status quo.

Depending on your past experiences, you may have to embrace change in order to survive in each new jungle you encounter. I had routinely been geared toward retention, and then I entered a realm where turnover is not only expected but often signals growth and innovation. In short, I found that I was changing faster than the people around me.

Soon I was to find that people who had been creative at one stage of growth now seemed empty of ideas—and worse, they seemed not to notice that the ground had moved up under their feet! As I grew and encountered higher ideals and new goals, what had once been acceptable now seemed lethargic at best and lethal if ignored.

You can't take everyone with you just because they were with you where you were before.

I felt divided. I couldn't decide whether to obey my heart or my mind!

I had to be savvy enough to realize the rules had changed and use my instincts to see how they changed.

Scare Me Again

How do we fight the complacency and paralysis of the past? How do we ignite our instincts? Several years ago, Joseph Garlington, a highly revered theologian and speaker from Pittsburgh, came to speak for us and shared an experience he had with his grandchildren.

As a grandfather myself, I can now relate to his story. Perhaps you've had those moments as well, when the children or grandchildren are bored playing alone and you are trying to read, research, study, or focus on a task before you. Subconsciously you notice they are skipping around, competing for your attention but not overtly.

Running up and down the stairs, they wait to catch your eye with their little feet fastened to the next step on the staircase. Finally, you look up from what you are doing and say, "Boo!" Screams of glee erupt from their lips like water from an artesian well. You go back to what you are doing, assuming that your exclamation of recognition will suffice. However, it is only a matter of time before you hear the tapping of happy feet again. They wait on the steps for you to look up again. And if you do not, the grandchild, weary of waiting, will exclaim, "Scare me again, Grandpa! Scare me again!"

That is what many gifted and talented people are waiting on: your instincts hunger for a task that is the equivalent to "Scare me again!" Make me study again. Challenge me with something special that will make me grow. Give me something challenging enough to make me think and work, create and develop.

I'm convinced the only way you can develop your true gifts, your creative instincts, is by embracing a vision so daunting that your heart goes running up the steps like a child, screaming with delight because you have a challenge that equals your creativity.

CHAPTER 7

Instincts Turned Inside Out

Instincts allow your internal vision to become an external reality. Often this process of actualization may involve unexpected and even unorthodox methods of discovery and application. I'll never forget the time when I was a boy and dressed myself for a very big event our family was attending. Normally, I would've gotten some assistance, but I've always been a bit precocious, and I really didn't think I needed help. Mother had already told me what to wear, I was a big boy, and I thought I knew what to do. So I reasoned, "I can handle this!" and proceeded to wiggle my way into my wardrobe.

Like any family with young children, of course we were running late, so I jumped in the backseat of the car, out of the view of my parents. I started to play with my siblings, which is always what the youngest does—torment the others, rather proud of myself for getting dressed without assistance. As we giggled and laughed, clowned and cut up, I never realized that the biggest laugh of the day was ultimately about to be on me.

Shortly after we arrived and were engulfed by the crowd, I heard some other children giggling at me. They began to point, and the sniggling grew. It seems I was fully dressed in what had been laid out for me, but my shirt was inside out. It didn't look that bad, but you know how children react to any little thing. Thoroughly humiliated in my childish embarrassment, I ran to my mother to fix the mess I made.

Now, being an adult, I fare much better at wearing my shirt the right way. Normally, I can manage to dress myself pretty well! Today's challenge is to get the once unintentional inside-out shirt to become a model for very intentional living. You see, I have come to understand that the art of being a visionary is to get the inside vision to materialize outside. Your instincts not only give voice to your innovative visions, but they transform mistakes into a mosaic masterpiece.

So often we look to others for inspiration, approval, or affirmation of what we should do and how we should do it. But you will never achieve the fulfillment of your vision this way. My friend, you are the singularly most effective source for outwardly manifesting all the visions, inventions, books, or businesses that are naturally part of your gifting. This explains why being copied is never an issue, since true creativity can never be synthesized.

Now, many can imitate what you do, but none can duplicate what you do if you produce outwardly what you possess inwardly. If you follow your instincts from the inside out, you emerge in a class all by yourself. You see, there is no one quite like you! You were not created to try and become the next Steve Jobs or Alice Walker or Nelson Mandela or Beyoncé!

You were created to bring something to this earth that has never crystallized throughout the eons of time. I don't know what that is for you, and you may not have fully discovered it yet, but if you live and lead by your instincts, your rare and precious gift—one of a kind—will emerge!

So stop manufacturing synthetic ideas or letting others pull your strings, and you won't have to fight off the competition. Put your seal, your scent, your essence, your DNA, on what you produce, and it will forever have that uniqueness. Stop copying and start discovering what is intrinsically within you.

Several years ago, I founded a festival called Megafest, an amalgamation of diverse interests of mine intersecting in one setting. My propensity for business themes and personal health merged with my passion for faith and spirituality. The very first year, over a hundred thousand people came from all walks of life to attend the event. Multiple countries and cultures were represented, and it was an unprecedented success.

However, the indelible moment of satisfaction that still lingers with me occurred the night before Megafest opened, as I marveled at how my vision had come to life. Without formal training or much experience, my team and I received international kudos for organizing such a massive undertaking with only a few minor glitches. More important, we were able to motivate, inspire, entertain, and invigorate a diverse body of people, encouraging and challenging them to enjoy the contentment that comes from living in the bull's-eye of their life's God-given goals. Through that first Megafest, I gained an even greater appreciation for what it means to actualize your instincts and live from the inside out.

Instinct Takes Inventory

Before you build a team, open a ministry, start a business, launch a concept, or develop a plan, you must begin to inventory what's on the inside of you. There is some powerful potion that's inherent in people who produce outwardly what is theirs. No, I didn't ask you what you could afford or what you studied at the university or seminary. I'm merely asking you to understand that instincts begin with inclinations that you may not have acted upon but should at least explore.

Just as it's possible to have never been exposed to a pool but be gifted as a swimmer, you may not have discovered your arena of greatness yet. Most creative, instinctive people ignite their passion by being exposed—sometimes even in the middle of their lives—to new ideas, other people, unusual positions, and unknown careers that they may not have encountered in their upbringing or normal environment. And yet they find themselves innately drawn to the beauty of a work of art, the brilliance of a new app, or the insight of fresh voices.

Scripture tells us that deep calls out to deep, and I'm convinced that those people, places, and perspectives that resonate with us often do so because of a shared, kindred quality. When something you encounter resonates with you, pay attention. Become a student of your deepest passions and most persistent curiosities. Notice the people you admire and feel drawn to emulate. We instinctively recognize members of our own tribe, no matter how different they may look!

Just because the goose lays eggs on land doesn't negate the fact that her offspring are drawn to the water. And the so-called ugly duckling often realizes they are really a swan in disguise! Can you go past where you started to discover what you could be? Listen to your instincts and you will find your power.

Our greatest power doesn't always emerge from our experiences, not even from our most intense ones. There's incredible hidden treasure locked up in your instincts that may not always show on your résumé. If you can spend some time with yourself, you may be on the verge of the most powerful part of your life, discovering what's inside that your instincts want to express outside.

Think about what you gravitate toward when given time to relax and recharge. Are you always watching cooking shows on the Food Network, tinkering with recipes to make them your own? Maybe you're exploring new apps, thinking about the ones you wish existed that you can't find. Do you find yourself perusing history books and travel brochures about a foreign land or culture that captivates you? Are you drawn to the latest leadership training course that's coming to town?

Paying attention to what nourishes and stimulates your heart, soul, and imagination leads to listening to your instincts. In turn, listening to your instincts jump-starts the process of creating the fabric of your destiny. Like a designer sewing a garment, you take the vision within you and bring it to life in a suit to be worn for your next season of life. You are instinctively best at inventing what is in your inventory!

Instinct Adapts

When you follow your instincts and transform your vision into reality, you will discover that accidents, mistakes, and conflicts become creative material. Rarely do you have everything you think you need in order to succeed. Living by instinct allows you to adapt to change and grow stronger. Instinct often processes, learns, and accepts change before we do. Once our emotions, intentions, and abilities catch up, we move forward, one step closer to seeing our dreams realized.

This idea began as a hypothesis in me and was affirmed as I deepened my research and discovered some compelling studies on the subjects of creativity and innovation. I've always believed that we are an extremely adaptable species. Our country's development reveals this adaptability in our founders' tenacious pursuit of creating a powerful new nation even amid the uncharted wilderness of a brand-new frontier—or at least it was new to them.

My ancestors modeled the concept of instinctive adaptability when they were snatched from their motherland and had to adapt to a world that was not only brutal but totally unfamiliar—new language, new faith, new foods, new customs, and new rules of engagement. I don't know how they survived such a hostile takeover of their heritage and culture. But they survived and adapted and endured.

I can see it in my own life as I have survived many changes of my worldview, catastrophic economic and health challenges, losses, disappointments, and moments of intense anguish. I have survived the magnanimous moments of intense accomplishments that catapulted me into strange new arenas for which I had no grooming or preparation. Trust me, both success and struggle are different kinds of trauma.

But at my core, I have always been a survivor. And though I may react to the trauma emotionally, shed private tears, have a meltdown away from people, or enjoy a complete "one flew over the cuckoo's nest" episode, when I'm finished expressing emotion I keep on keeping on. When I finish my rant, tantrum, or moment of grief, I move into the instinctive survival mode that has empowered humans to endure plights and pleasures of all kinds. Change is often as painful for me to endure as it is for anyone else, but I have learned to take the bitter with the sweet and keep on moving forward.

Everything I have been able to accomplish and most of the exceptional accomplishments of others I've witnessed result from something that's hardwired into our cores. Some download better than others, but I believe all of us have more talents stocked in our inventory than life's demands have required from us. It could be that oppositions and opportunities alike challenge us to draw from our inventory that which we might've been oblivious to otherwise. Think of how many things you had in you that required a challenge or a change to help you discover, utilize, and embrace.

Instinct Inspires

As I've researched adaptability, I've discovered some critical information on what I see as a pattern. Science teaches us that the role of instincts in determining behavior of animals varies from species to species. It appears that the more complex the neural system of the animal, the less that species is inclined to rely on instincts.

Generally, from a biological perspective, the greater the role of the cerebral cortex—which draws on sociological constructs for learning—the less instinctive the creature becomes. Both its defenses and needs are accomplished by its supreme ability to deduce and decide. It doesn't have to rely on instincts, because of its biological neural system. It isn't that the instincts aren't there. They are simply not the primary resource for rescue and resiliency.

With this in mind, I wonder if this in fact describes what has happened with us as we react to life in the twenty-first century. Some people live and lead from their instincts, but most of us rely on intellect, social conditioning, and logic. Myriad voices scream at us daily from every source imaginable, and we sadly become deafened to the whispers of our own instincts.

Perhaps in a perfect world working with someone fully engaged with both would be a dream. They would regard facts but not ignore feelings, either. They could censor data meticulously but also have creative instincts capable of overriding what may seem logical on paper but impractical in execution.

This is the opiate of advancement. It liberates the soul to escape the obvious when need be and break beyond the historical orthodoxy of the previously held ideology. Through this union of timely information and the creative impulse of the instinct, we forge ahead into new excursions of ideas!

Yes, we all have instincts, intuition, and internal discernment. However, some never allow the activation of what is on the inside. Some people maintain that our intellects should eclipse our instincts. They have even suggested that the more cerebral we are, the less we benefit from relying on instincts. Nothing could be further from the truth.

Sometimes we've deadened the nerve endings of our instincts by indulging in the luxury of deciding by the numbers and living in the books instead of creating in the crosshairs of crisis. We don't use what we think we don't need. And as long as what we have been taught provides for us, why would we look deeper to unleash the many other gifts that are intrinsically stocked within all of us?

Recently I toured Nike headquarters, and one of the displays had a tennis shoe stuck in a waffle iron. The company's cofounder, Phil Knight, had partnered with a guy named Bill Bowerman, and they each contributed $500 to start the company! In the early years of the company, Bowerman was inspired by a waffle iron to develop a sole for better running, with less weight and more traction. Who could've imagined that a waffle-iron-inspired running shoe would become an iconic, international brand? How's that for out of the box!

Our instincts inspire us to look beyond the usual and identify the unusual. If we're attuned, our instincts transfer principles from one field of study to another, mix metaphors that yield new insights, and create fresh designs from tired traditions. Our instincts identify relationships among disparate people, places, and principles before we do. They spot patterns, designs, and threads of commonality.

Bowerman saw a waffle iron and a tennis shoe and married them into a multibillion-dollar corporation! Just consider how many people had been exposed to the waffle iron and had seen tennis shoes but didn't have the instinct to converge the two concepts. Can you imagine going to the bank and saying, "I have an idea from a waffle iron that is going to make me rich"? There was no intelligence to support it. There was no data to refer to. The risk was built on an instinct that paid off with unprecedented success.

Once you have confidence in your instincts, you must never allow other people's refusal to believe, or their data to refute, what you instinctively know is true. Your instincts know the blueprint for success that's within you and how to bring it to life all around you. Don't give up or be deterred from your destiny just because it doesn't seem to fit a formula. As we say in Texas, "If you believe there's a fox in that hole, point your tail and keep on barking!"

CHAPTER 8

✦

Instincts to Increase

O ur human instincts transcend physical survival and
include our unique gifting and purpose. When we
unleash our instincts to guide us, we discover the special
ways we've been equipped, educated, and enlightened to
fulfill our destiny. Your instincts are more resourceful,
resilient, and responsive than you probably realize.

So many tell me that they know what they were
designed to do but simply can't catch a break. They tell
me that their circumstances limit them, their finances
prohibit them, and their relationships inhibit them.
When you unleash your instincts, though, you will
find a way to move through, up, over, and beyond what
appears to prevent your progress.

When ideas hang out with influence, income will
always emerge. Most people abort their creative, out-of-
the-box ideas for fear of the investment. But a great idea

can attract investors. I have always believed that relationships are our greatest resource. But those relationships must cross-pollinate beyond the familiar. You must not limit yourself to any one singular viewpoint. You need a manufacturer in the room with a senator, a record producer next to the record breaker, a scientist alongside the artist, the banker teamed with a lawyer. Over the years I've learned you can't be surrounded with monolithic relationships and tap into a full release of your potential. I remain a great believer in research and data, but at the end of the day, most great discoveries can be traced back to instincts.

So when I have an instinctive idea, it will die in the crib if I don't assemble a team around it that has similar instincts but diverse perspectives of influence and contribution. The best way to kill your instincts is to surround yourself with only practical people who never take the voyage beyond what the empirical data states. If you only move based on data, you will only regurgitate old ideas. Refer to the data and heed its wisdom when feasible, but sooner or later, all inventors and most investors must cut through the clutter of quarterly reports and ground themselves in their instincts.

And when creative instincts emerge, resources will eventually catch up. Usually, the information has to play catch-up with the inclination. You aren't one bank loan away from a million dollars, but you are one creative idea from a million dollars. When circumstances seem to hold you hostage, your instincts pay the ransom.

At its core an instinct is an inborn pattern of activity or tendency to act that's common to a given species. It is also a natural or an innate impulse or inclination. These instincts are not just the basic ones you might consider, such as for survival, procreation, or fight-or-flight.

In my research, I was surprised to discover that some experts believe many people possess an instinct or a natural aptitude for making money, others for healing, creating art, organizing, or negotiating. I'm convinced our instincts emerge out of and alongside our gifting, so it makes sense that our instincts would reflect our talents and abilities.

As one expert from Wikipedia explains, "Any behavior is instinctive if it is performed without being based upon prior experience (that is, in the absence of learning), and is therefore an expression of innate biological factors. For example, sea turtles, newly hatched on a beach, will automatically move toward the ocean. A joey climbs into its mother's pouch upon being born. Honeybees communicate by dancing in the direction of a food source without formal instruction."

Roar of the Entrepreneur

Regardless of our particular instincts, they all share a common direction: forward. Going out into the wild frontier of possibilities means you have to wean yourself from the nurturing state of normal and accepted practices. All of life is available to us, but not everyone will go through what it takes to enlarge our lives and reshape our environment so that we can release our instincts.

Visit your local zoo, and there you will see animals living in cages. As long as the animal—say, a lion—stays in the cage, he knows exactly when he will eat. Cages are comfortable. Cages are consistent. They provide security. And generally they are safe. And yet I suspect there's often an alluring urge within our golden-maned friend in a cage to see what's beyond the safety of his warm bed and conveniently placed water trough in the cage's corner.

For the animal born in captivity, there's no basis for comparison. His needs are met and he is safe. "Isn't that enough?" many may ask. But if the cage were truly natural, then why must it remain locked? Keepers lock cages because animals are instinctively drawn to the wild, even if they have never lived in the wilderness. The lion longs for something he may never have experienced, even when his needs are met in the cage.

This is the roar of the entrepreneur. It's not that she can't get a job and be safe. It is that she is attracted to the frontier beyond the cage. The comfort of present limitations may be safe, but where there's nothing ventured, there's of course nothing gained. Most creative innovators eventually migrate from the familiar cage of controlled environments into the wild and, yes, dangerous frontier of entrepreneurship.

Whatever tickles your instincts, it will be something powerful and persistent. Regardless of where your instincts may lead, the question remains the same. Do you have the courage to adapt to the wild after living in the cage? Or to put it another way, what do you do when your experiences conflict with your instincts? What if you're raised in the ghetto but have instincts for the suburbs? It's the lion's dilemma. If you were trained for a job but have the longing to be an entrepreneur, you feel his pain. If you long to be in a loving, stable relationship but have only known breakups and heartbreak, then you see through the lion's eyes.

The jungle beckons but the cage comforts.

Even after the decision to take the risk has been made, the struggle is far from over. In many ways, it's just begun. If for some reason this animal, which was never created to be caged but has been all of his life, is placed in his natural habitat—the jungle that he was always meant to be in—he may die.

Although his instincts still reside within and will eventually surface, this transition into the wild may be difficult or fatal if his natural instincts are not reawakened and gradually restored. Leaving a cage for the opportunity to discover the freedom of your true identity requires not only leaving the safety behind bars, but also learning to harness the wilderness within.

What is natural may not feel normal, because your experiences don't match your inclinations. Just because something is natural doesn't means it feels normal when you have never had an opportunity to explore the true essence of your instincts.

Cages and Stages

Imagine how important it is that we wean the lion from the cycles of the cage and gradually reintroduce him to the primal sensation of freedom. That alluring gaze at freedom from a structured job or career may tantalize you with the notion of being your own boss. But I must warn you that the sensual notion of freedom can be a seductive trap if you don't understand that you are stepping into a world that isn't as carefree as it looks.

New predators, new diets, and new abodes await you. You will have to learn to hunt your own prey and avoid being someone else's. Though many of us aren't happy in cages and feel drawn to the wild, we must never underestimate the fierceness of freedom and the danger of the new world of self-fulfillment.

Instinctively successful individuals almost always have had to go through a metamorphosis in order to free themselves from their cagelike habits. And more important, they need time and training to adapt and to develop the instincts that are critical to survive in the new environment. If the lion needs that adaption space to develop a more natural instinct, we, too, have to be prepared to be mentored and tutored even when we possess the instinct to increase.

The unborn baby lies in a cage we call a womb. He has eyes but cannot use them, and a mouth that he has never eaten with. He has been innately equipped for a world he has not been exposed to. His innate instincts like sucking, seeing, walking, and sitting have never been utilized because no opportunity exists in his present safe and warm cocoon of development. He must be born and enter the world to discover the instincts imbued by his Creator.

Cages and wombs come in all kinds of shapes and sizes. It doesn't have to be a dead-end job to be a cage. It can be renting as opposed to owning a home. For some it is the desperate clinging to singleness for fear of the heart-racing perils of intimate partnership. Many would rather sit at a table for one than risk the awkwardness of bolting into the uncertainty of coupling. In that new cycle of circumstances the cost of admission is the risk of rejection and abandonment. We all have cages of comfort that protect us but also isolate us from discovering not only what lies outside but also what lies within.

The baby cannot grow and mature into a healthy child until he leaves the womb. He is finally birthed into something bigger, and it is only after the cord is cut that he discovers within himself unused instruments that have only just become activated. I fully believe that many people never really leave the wombs of simple survival to the bigger world beyond. Now, you must understand that birthing is traumatic.

Over and over we repeat the process. We go from the womb to the family, which is also a controlled environment that feeds and sustains us. By the time we adapt to our family, we are birthed into the world around us, and we have to activate instincts of survival or return to the cage of living at home again!

Could it be that the social constructs of Mommy and Daddy only lead to the jungle of high school? The baby becomes the toddler becomes the child becomes the tween becomes the teenager. Each stage includes its own weaning into the next phase. Often the adolescent leaves the family bruised by the assault of rebellion as he tries to escape the identity of "Who am I to the family?" and into the wild of "Who am I to myself?"

The rebellion so prevalent at that age is the flailing cry of an emerging adult struggling to go where his instincts demand but mortified at the same time by the wilderness of the second womb vacated. The diploma is awarded, the cord is cut, and with a vehicle for vacating the home, he opens the door to the wild! But is he ready?

Welcome to the jungle of mating instincts, Facebook friends, and the ferocious and foreign prospects of public performance. Independent environments now require that he disengage some behaviors that he developed within his last environment and develop instincts that will enable him to survive in the wild.

Instinct to Jump

Now, some are pushed but some fear the low-grade life of playing it safe and jump into a waiting destiny they sense deep within. And, yes, it takes a certain kind of person to risk in this way. Curiously enough, these types become the people we end up reading about, watching on television, listening to on our iPods, and following on Twitter. They are what I call jumpers—people willing to jump out of their nests, or run out of their cages and into the free fall of the jungle, where they must survive by their instincts.

Recently I encountered a quotation from a famous jumper that sums up his instinctive philosophy on life: "Your time is limited, so don't waste it living someone else's life. Don't be trapped by dogma—which is living with the results of other people's thinking. Don't let the noise of others' opinions drown out your own inner voice. And most important, have the courage to follow your heart and your intuition. They somehow already know what you truly want to become. Everything else is secondary."

This statement comes from Steve Jobs, the visionary founder of Apple, recently declared the most recognizable brand in the world, surpassing Coca-Cola for the first time ever. You know where I encountered Mr. Jobs' sage advice? On P. Diddy's Instagram! As crazy as it sounds to consider what Steve Jobs, Sean Combs, and T.D. Jakes have in common, if nothing else we are all jumpers! We have each risked leaving our cages and venturing out into the wilds to discover how our dreams can be brought to life.

Let me give you another example. Bob Johnson, who built up Black Entertainment Television (BET) into a multi-million-dollar enterprise, could not remain content with his achievements. After investing his time, energy, and resources into the unqualified success of BET, what did he do next? He sold it!

He realized what everyone willing to leave the cage eventually realizes—entering the jungle is not a one-time event. Certainly, when he first entered television and considered the prospect of starting a new cable channel geared toward African-Americans, Mr. Johnson probably felt like he had entered a jungle. And yet, years later what once seemed like a jungle had become another cage.

So Bob Johnson entered a new jungle of even wilder endeavors—purchasing the Charlotte Bobcats, which he later sold to Michael Jordan—another jumper and then some! Real estate, investments, asset management, and philanthropy became jungles for

Mr. Johnson as well. Based on his willingness to enter jungle after jungle, it's no wonder then that Bob Johnson became the first black billionaire in our country.

He knows what all eagles in the air know. It's okay to be fearful, but don't let the fear keep you from flying! And the rush of adrenaline that comes from overcoming one's fears is addictive. When you leave the familiar and enter the unknown, your fear becomes refined by experience and hammered into tools of survival on the anvil of anxiety.

I am never more passionate about a fight than when I fear my opponent. Fear teaches you to be cautious, careful, and conscientious. It also forces you to be creative, compassionate, and calculating. So often, fear becomes the fuel for your power in the jungle. As my friend Joyce Meyer says, "Feel the fear and do it anyway!"

CHAPTER 9

⊷◇⊷

Instincts Under Pressure

Instincts under pressure crush the carbon of conformity and create diamonds. Each new season of life offers to train us for the next season if we pay attention and adapt. If in this training camp we call life, we learned to survive with a job and that is how we received the nourishment of income, when something happens to that job we are thrown into the wild of unemployment. This adaption feels much like the caged animal sent to the jungle. We ask, "How do I eat in this environment? What do I do next? How do I protect myself and my family?"

When we are placed in a set of circumstances where we have to take initiative and be creative, some of us find it hard to transition. Those people have been trained not to think but to obey orders. They are slaves to the training, unconsciously pledging allegiance to the average. Mentally they recite from the manual of mediocrity.

But how quickly they discover that the old rules don't often apply. In other words, they must adapt. They must become a quick study or risk becoming some predator's entrée! It's not a matter of intelligence but of instinctive adaptability, which means you may not have the past training or experience to prepare you for these new challenges. But if you do not immediately recognize the vast changes in your environmental circumstances, then the opportunity for growth and innovative achievement closes.

You could be a leader and not know it. You could be a warm, loving person innately but not have had an opportunity to unpack what's inside of you. You could be an artist, a parent, a healer, a communicator and simply not have had the opportunity for adaptation yet.

Transitions are usually challenging. But what is exciting is that though we often resist, complain, or become irritable and cry like babies, we do so because we have the confusion of being unsettled and forced to discover new skill sets. If we are willing to trust our instincts and act on them, most of us can adapt and reacclimatize to the new social constructs we are placed in. I'm convinced at our core we are ultimately survivors, constantly thrust into new jungles and perpetually rediscovering dormant capabilities we didn't realize lay within us.

The fact that you may be experiencing trouble activating those internal instincts necessary for transition simply doesn't mean that you don't have it in you to do so. You must realize that no matter how gifted you were at receiving income one way, it doesn't mean that you can't unearth the creativity and passion to receive it another way. Or the fact that you haven't lived alone for years doesn't mean you can't cast off the learned behavior of a previous relationship and find your instinct to be contented in another social construct.

Ever wonder what your life would be like if you stepped outside of what people expect from you? Isn't it time to step outside the cage and find out? What if you discovered something previously undiscovered, something God placed inside of you to fuel your purpose in life?

Our Creator has gifted you with varied tools for survival both intellectually and instinctively. Survival in life will require that you use them all. What you activate in one set of circumstances may now have to be overridden to adapt to a new set of circumstances. But you do have the gift, the ability, and the elasticity of internal fortitude to unearth those skill sets that are necessary for change and implement them for the next move.

The Hell of Regret

He who wins the race cannot run with the pack. And once you get out you can't come back, because caged lions don't mate with free ones! If ever you are going to win, you must forsake the social construct of the cage and all the cage dwellers. Whether they are business associates, community activists, political pundits, or any other order that has spoken and unspoken rules, you will have to take your own stand. This is never easy.

I cannot tell you how many times I have been that animal who hears the sound of the gate creaking open and momentarily freezes in place. And then with a racing heart, I step into a world where the first terrifying sound I hear is the same gate closing shut behind me. So many times I have not known the lay of the land I was about to explore, but I knew that the passage behind me had closed forever.

This rattles the nerves. And yet, we must consider facing our fears and asking what we will regret the most. I'm not as afraid of dying as many people. I learned early that death is a part of life. My greatest fear is not living before I die, to play everything so safe that even though I had no risk I also enjoyed no reward.

You see, the Olympic race of fear within you has but two contenders. One is the claustrophobic fear of staying, and the other contestant is the heart-pounding, adrenaline-releasing fear of stepping into the unknown world before you. This race is especially close when instincts take you where your history forsakes you. And there you are left alone with the frightening prospects of that which feels foreign and yet entices the instincts within.

You see, I am afraid of spending my whole life with

the deceptive deduction that my cage is the world! So when death tolls and life's final buzzer shrilly ends my tournament, more tragic than the end of the temporal would be the eternal hypotheticals of "what if?" When I consider such a fate, the hell of regret singes my soul. The agonizing anguish of wondering what I might've been or done if I'd had the courage to free myself from learned behaviors and the cages life imposes is indeed the wind beneath my wings!

I'm not talking about just the cages of calling and careers but something much more significant: the cage of contained thought. The sanctity of the orthodox, succumbing to living in the land of the average, seems a massive waste of will and wit.

Instinct Likes a Challenge

We're used to basing our decisions on past experiences and then suddenly our instincts pull us toward something equally tantalizing and terrifying. We cannot deny our instinctive attraction, and yet we're unsettled by its unfamiliarity. Nothing in our repertoire of achievements and abilities, nor our family, our training, our education, or our experiences has prepared us, and yet we are drawn instinctively toward something that excites us, touches us, energizes us, and leaves us shaking in our boots.

From my experiences and those of many others,

instinct likes a challenge more than it likes comfort. Our instincts would rather lead us to face the unknown than let us shrink into the corner of our cage. When we're committed to fulfilling our destiny, our instinct drives us away from complacency and toward contentment.

An inmate leaving prison must certainly feel this odd mixture of excitement and fear as he walks through the door of his cell one last time, through the gates of the prison grounds. What had become familiar to him, normal and routine, must now be left behind. He must start over. And as exhilarated as he may be by the restoration of his freedom, he also must make his way into a new jungle that has grown unrecognizable from when he knew it before. In fact, many parolees and former inmates become so stressed trying to reacclimate to the outside that they often end up returning to crime.

Did they commit a crime in hopes of returning to the confinement of a prison cell? Probably not consciously, but one wonders when looking at the recidivism rate. The literal, physical incarceration may even seem preferable to the fear of learning to live outside the prison walls.

Even if we have never faced physical confinement, most of us can relate. It doesn't matter whether it's a new career, a new marriage, a new season of being single, a new business launch. When we start anything by following our instincts, we will likely be forced to leave our cage of comfort and complacency.

Everything's Bigger in Texas

I faced this very dilemma when I made the decision to move my family and ministry from Charleston, West Virginia, where I'd grown up and lived all my life, to Dallas, Texas, which I probably knew better from television and movies than from my own experience. I'm still not exactly sure how it came about. I became interested in the Dallas area because I had heard that many people there attended church regularly (not always the case in urban areas) and were open to joining a new Christian community. I had also heard that property was relatively affordable for such a large urban area.

Ironically enough, I had actually told a friend of mine, another pastor, that he ought to move to Dallas and start a church there. But after some thoughtful and prayerful consideration, he ended up going another direction. And yet the thought of this place I had recommended to him haunted me. I began to wonder what Dallas was really like. While I had been through there a time or two, I knew very little about the people, the culture, the flavor and lifestyle of Texans. And yet I couldn't quit thinking about moving to the Dallas–Fort Worth area. It remained an alluring attraction, one I finally could not ignore.

When I went to Dallas and visited the prospective property for a new church, I asked the owner if I could have a few minutes alone in the building and he agreed. There in the echoing cavern of a structure so much larger than our entire church back in West Virginia, I asked God if this was where he wanted me. It didn't take long before my awareness of his presence increased, and everything in me heard, "Yes."

Even with this sense of God's calling and blessing upon the move, I remained fearful. I had lived in West Virginia my entire life! I would not only be leaving my church to plant a new one, but I would be leaving one lifestyle and culture for another. The Dallas–Fort Worth metropolitan area included over two million people at that time—about twenty times more than Charleston! And how would Texans take to an African-American outsider moving into their territory? If everything is bigger in Texas, would that include prejudice and hostility?

With growing trepidation, I agonized over this decision. I paced the cage that contained me and wondered if I dared set foot into the Texan jungle opening before me. If I stayed put, would I regret not exploring this opportunity, forever wondering, "What if…?" Or would I long for the comfortable security of my humble roots and regret my risk when inevitably confronted with adversity?

Moving away would include uprooting my wife and kids, and taking my mother with us after she had lived over six decades in the same area. We would be leaving the small-town warmth of our cocooned community and launching out on new wings. But would we fly? Or flutter momentarily before crashing to the ground?

It was a huge risk, but I had to take it. I had to leave my cage. Not only did I feel God's prompting to make the move, but something deep inside me knew it was where I belonged—even if I didn't exactly know why. Needless to say, I have never regretted my decision to follow my instincts and move to Dallas. No, instead I discovered that my move was not just an open door to me but was in fact the intersection of the destiny of thousands if not millions of others whose lives would forever be changed, all predicated upon me releasing my fear and mustering the courage to be stretched beyond my comfort.

Instinct to Fly

When we find ourselves at the crossroads between at least two different directions, we often panic. It feels like a no-win. After our instincts have been stirred by a vision, a glimpse, a divine whisper inside us, we cannot ignore the decision. Or, if we do, then that in itself becomes a decision we know we will soon regret. When our instincts magnetically urge us in a particular direction, my experience has been that we will regret not acting on that urge. Standing at the crossroads may feel like being caught in the crosshairs!

But I'm convinced that it is so much more productive, satisfying, and invigorating to have risked a new endeavor and failed than to play it safe and remain in the status quo. When a mother eagle senses instinctively that her eaglets are now ready to fly, she disrupts the nest with her beak, pushing them out with an eviction notice that seems so cruel. Her beak dislodges them from their nest and pushes them to the edge. Have you ever been pushed to the edge?

I saw eagles in the plain I visited soaring in the wind. It was amazing to me to realize that what seems so natural now was once a moment of great terror. When it was young that eagle was pushed to the edge. Its mother's beak had no doubt dropped him off the edge of the cliff!

The results produce a striking beauty, but in the moment of crossing from nest to nature, the sight would make you call the animal rights commission and file a complaint of abuse! The mother obviously is not being cruel to her little birds. Instead she is pushing them into the uncomfortable place of discovery. She knows that the nest was only the crossroads through which they would grow and develop. If they sat in the temporary, it would be at the expense of the permanent.

Now, I'm told the little birds become frightened half to death and initially start flapping their wings out of terror, flailing wildly to ward off what looks like inevitable death. But the flailing of their fear is the birthing of a discovery. Their instinct to fly is released with great peril and fear.

In the galing winds and impending danger, they find that the wings they never utilized in their previous comfortable nest find use in the fall and give birth to their flight. To ensure that they will not come back to the nest, she stirs the nest with her beak so that the prickly briars protrude and make it impossible for them to find comfort where they once rested.

I can't tell you how many times I've been forced to find my wings by the discomfort of staying where I was. I've felt like an eaglet more than once, forced out many times by circumstances I couldn't control. I've screamed inwardly a thousand reasons why the time wasn't right or I wasn't prepared. If you are like me, you tell yourself, "But I don't have the experience or the training or the education or the relationships or the resources necessary to take such a dangerous leap!"

All of which may be true. But there are times when we must disregard the data and distance our doubts if we are ever going to achieve greater velocity toward the goals that roar within us. We must follow our instinct to fly.

CHAPTER 10

⬛◇⬛

Instincts Set the Pace

Once you've overcome some of your fears and left the cage (or the nest), you must keep flying. Once you've conquered certain limitations, you never stop. The dreams may get bigger, the challenges more daunting, the opportunities more thrilling, but your journey in the wild of life never ends. Once you've mastered the new wild, it eventually seems too domestic. It gives way to new opportunities and the next wild is always before you.

However, sometimes the key to following your instincts to the next level of success is all in the timing. It's not only a matter of when you jump, but your pace as you transition to the next new jungle. Or, think of it this way: eagles may be jumpers but lions are not! Sometimes we must stroll out of the cage gradually rather than jump into the jungle suddenly.

When trainers introduce domesticated lions back into the wild, they do so in incremental steps. The lions leave their cages and spend time in their natural habitat before returning to the cages, then venture out for a longer duration on their next excursion with the trainers. Eventually, they remain in the wild and never return to the domesticated home that once enclosed them.

This model works equally as well and is obviously more cautious and perhaps more practical for many people wanting to follow their instincts out of the cage. Please understand that I do not advocate taking foolish risks and closing doors and burning bridges without some semblance of support from which to draw your sustenance. It's one thing to take a huge risk, but it's another thing to live in the jungle on the first day!

So sometimes we stroll out of our cage, explore the terrain, return to our cage for a while, explore the jungle again, and so on until we can navigate the wilderness and forge some semblance of a way forward. To put it another way, we must look ahead and anticipate what we can handle. Scripture tells us that we must count the cost before we build our house, and the same is true with leaving the cage. If you know you don't have resources to support you for the first year and beyond, then don't quit your job to explore the jungle of your instinctive passion. Instead, start a side business or take a class; find a mentor or volunteer in an organization centered on your interests.

This is a safer model of leaving your cage and it balances the external realities of your responsibilities with the relentless longing of your internal instincts. When you take baby steps, you discover the strength of your legs before you try to run. You're still on a high wire, but there's a safety net if you fall.

While I've done my share of jumping, I've also practiced this more gradual method. When we moved to Dallas, for the first couple months I continued to preach at my church in West Virginia before flying to my new church home and preaching there. Many weekends, I would be in a pulpit in Charleston on Sunday morning and in another pulpit in Dallas on Sunday night. It wasn't easy, but it provided a bit of a safety net as I prepared to leave the security of my past life behind.

You can be wholehearted in pursuing where your instincts are leading you and still be practical. Please understand that following your instincts does not mean you have to make a dramatic departure from everything that you currently consider your cage. My friends in publishing tell me how many people they encounter who quit their day jobs so that they can write best sellers—even though they know nothing about publishing and very little about writing!

Similarly, my friends in the music world describe

individuals who leave everything behind and yet have not prepared themselves for the realities of their new jungle as they compete for performance opportunities and producers' attention. So look before you leap. Sometimes it's better to remain in the cage until after feeding time rather than risk starving in the jungle!

It's perfectly normal to be terrified of making changes. And it's perfectly normal to stumble, fall, and have to get up again and again as you make your way through your new environment. However, don't rush when you don't have to! And don't burn bridges behind you—enough of them will catch fire by themselves! When you lose your job, then you have no choice but to enter the jungle. But if you don't have to shut the door of the cage, then leave it cracked open so that you can retreat there as needed.

No Turning Back

As terrifying as it may be, sometimes the best thing in the world that can happen to us is for the cage door to slam shut. When the door closes on yesterday, we must bring our energies to today. When we can't go back, then we're forced to go forward! Without the safety of the cage tempting us to reverse course, we must bring all that we are—our creativity, resiliency, innovation, and resourcefulness—to our new jungle.

One of the best things that ever happened to the Children of Israel was when God closed the Red Sea after their triumphant exodus out of Egypt. The water opened before them so that they could escape, but it also closed behind them, preventing them from returning. And later, over the course of the forty years it took them to reach the Promised Land, many of them grumbled and complained that their lives were better back in Egypt—despite the fact that they had been slaves there! But reaching this point of no return required them to depend on God, his provision, and one another in ways that returning to Egypt—or going immediately to the Promised Land—never could have achieved.

When I decided to bring Megafest to Dallas recently, I faced scary, uncharted waters of my own. It had been over five years since the previous Megafest in Atlanta, and so much had changed. Over 50 percent of the staff that had assisted in Atlanta had moved on to new opportunities and new locales. The majority of the members of my church had not witnessed or experienced Megafest from the inside out.

So many questions, many logistical, loomed before me as I prepared to bring this spectacular event to the place I now call home. Could the public transportation systems adequately handle the influx of tens and even hundreds of thousands of people? Atlanta has long had its MARTA public transit system, which worked quite effectively at transporting attendees to our venues, but would Dallas's DART system handle the influx just as well?

Atlanta drew many people from the South, East, and Midwest because it was within a day's driving distance from Charlotte, Birmingham, Nashville, and Jacksonville. The same would not be true for these people when coming to Dallas. Would they still come?

Many people saw that we were holding Megafest in Dallas and assumed it was a slam-dunk, no-brainer kind of decision. But what many failed to realize is that I felt more vulnerable, more afraid, more insecure hosting it here than anywhere else! If it flopped, it would be in my own backyard; its flaws would be front and center for all who knew me best—my church, my community, and my city. This was vulnerability times ten!

So my team and I took nothing for granted. We worked harder and longer to make Megafest in Dallas a bigger success than we had before in Atlanta. Leading up to the event, I traveled and promoted it extensively: London, Australia, New York, Chicago, and across our country. I conducted media interviews with the *Today* show, *Entertainment Tonight*, and every major newspaper, magazine, and online site that would have me. I knew I had to do everything in my power to ensure success; I could take nothing for granted—certainly not past successes.

When there's no turning back, your instincts will lead you forward.

Stumble Toward Success

As you leave the cage, the transition into the jungle will definitely be challenging. You take a few steps forward and a few back. You stumble and fall and get back on your feet. Such is the way we learn to lean forward and keep stumbling toward success. For the newborn baby, as well as for a first-time mother, those first attempts at nursing can end in painful disappointment for both. The baby has to learn how to receive nourishment from the nipple when it is offered. The mother has to learn patience and stamina as she passes the nutrients of her milk to her child.

In other words, it is totally normal to struggle as you leave the cage and acclimate to the new wilderness before you. Toddlers typically stumble, bumble, and trip before learning to walk. But they keep getting back on their feet and tottering forward until they no longer have to think about keeping their balance. Similarly, when learning to ride a bicycle, whether it be as a child or an adult, one is bound to lose control and crash until the complexity of simultaneous skills becomes second nature.

Many people do not get admitted to college, pass the bar, or become licensed in their field until after several failed attempts. But they persevere, undeterred, wiser and more committed to achieving their goal than they were during the previous attempt. My mama always said, "The world is our university and everyone you encounter is your teacher. When you wake up each day, make sure you go to school!"

It's not how many times you have failed; it's what you've learned each time you got back on your feet. Did losing that job a few years ago help you discover the kind of work environment where you can thrive? Did auditioning for that role you didn't get make you more determined to practice harder the next time? Did declaring bankruptcy for your home business enable you to manage your finances better for your new company? Each time you fail, there's a clue to your future success.

We need to fail boldly if we want to succeed extravagantly! So often successful people do not reveal their failures—and why should they? We cannot fault them for not wanting to make their mistakes front and center, especially when they have clearly overcome those obstacles to reach the summits of their particular mountains. But we must remember that the person whizzing by you as you struggle to keep pedaling has just as many skinned knees as you do! Successful people follow their instincts beyond the emotions of their failures.

Instincts Transform Failures

Let me share one of the most educational experiences of my life—or, to put it another way, one of my most spectacular flops! Early in my career as a pastor, I decided to stage a production of my Gospel play based on my book, *Woman, Thou Art Loosed!,* and take it on tour. Talk about a comedy of errors! Just about everything that could go wrong did go wrong!

I was trying to preach at the same time the show was going up, dividing my attention and keeping me stressed on stage and in the pulpit. Rehearsals were disastrous, and the blocking seemed clumsy and awkward. Ticket sales were so poor that we had to give away a large number at the last minute to fill the auditoriums we'd booked. I soon realized I had hired the wrong people and ended up having to fire some of them the same week we opened.

There was simply so much I did not know about how to open a show and take it on the road. I didn't know that you open it in small markets to work out the kinks before taking it into large cities. I had no clue how to effectively market and promote this kind of dramatic endeavor. I didn't know which people to hire and which to avoid, or which venues were better than others and which to avoid altogether because of how they'd scalp you!

This experience presented a great opportunity to give

up. I had invested my own money in it and couldn't afford to keep it going for long. I couldn't afford to ascend the steep learning curve that continued to loom before me. And yet...I couldn't afford to quit. I loved seeing a story inside my imagination come to life on the stage. I felt compelled to share a message with an audience hungry for hope. It wasn't just the financial and emotional investment in the show; it was the investment in my future I could not afford to give up.

So I knew I had to find a way to keep going, one way or another. You've heard the saying "fake it 'til you make it"? Well, I "faithed" it 'til I made it! I learned the hard way how to make cast changes at the last minute and how to market plays and sell tickets so that the cast could get paid. I learned about lighting, music, theater acoustics, and the difference between amateur and professional actors.

I also met a young playwright and actor named Tyler Perry who was touring with a play of his own, *I Know I've Been Changed*. After being so amazed at his dexterity with language, storytelling, and acting, I requested a meeting with him and asked him to help me with the script for my own play. He graciously agreed, and we formed a friendship and professional relationship that continues to this day.

Through working with Tyler, I realized that often when you're laboring to come out of the cage, you must follow someone who's already a few paces ahead of you. These other risk takers already know where to find water, where to look for food, and who to avoid in the jungle. They will often help you if you ask and allow them to impart the wisdom they've acquired in the wild.

As you can see, I learned so much from that string of painful mistakes and frustrating miscues. Should I have quit after that first disastrous run? Probably! But could I quit? No, my instincts wouldn't allow it.

And for good reason. Then I could never have imagined that now, over three decades later, I would be making films, consulting on scripts, casting, filming locations, and budgets. The exhilaration I felt at the premiere of my first major movie, *Woman, Thou Art Loosed*, could never have occurred if I had given up. If I had followed logic, I would have lost so much more than the education that can only come from mistakes and the school of hard knocks. Following my instincts, even through what felt like the valley of the shadow but was actually just a new jungle, led me to the fulfillment of my gifts.

All Eyes on You

I'll never forget being on safari and sitting out under the night sky with thousands of diamondlike stars glistening brightly above us. Since there were no artificial lighting sources—no streetlights, skyscrapers, billboards, or shopping malls—the dark seemed thicker and deeper, which only made the starlight seem brighter.

There were faint sounds occasionally from the bush surrounding us, but overall it felt peaceful and relatively quiet. That is, until our guide shone his flashlight in a 360-degree sweep around our campsite! As his beam penetrated the surrounding foliage of the African bush, dozens of luminescent eyes glared back at us. It's one thing to know those creatures are out there, but I'm telling you it's another to have them staring back at you! They were watching us, scrutinizing our every move, prepared to fight or flee depending on our actions.

Once you leave your cage, you, too, will be watched and scrutinized by dozens of people. As you become uncaged and integrated into your latest jungle, there will be plenty of naysayers, critics, and skeptics. But keep in mind, like the eyes shining back at us on my safari, most of them will not physically hurt you. They may frighten you and make a lot of noise and increase your anxiety, but ultimately, you must ignore their stares and remain focused on creating your own path.

Once you enter the jungle of your new endeavor, some people will be jealous while others will feel threatened or intimidated. Some will want to compete and compare, and others will try to cover and capture. In the midst of such adversity, you must sidestep the dangers they present and follow your own instincts.

When others offer advice, criticism, or instruction,

you should listen, consider it, and keep it in mind. But ultimately, you can only follow your own instincts and not someone else's. Steve Jobs was right. You must never live anyone else's life but your own. You must fly on your own two wings!

CHAPTER 11

Instinctive Investments

When you follow your instincts, you invest in your future success. As I've shared, this instinct to increase is not about dollars but about dreams. Not that the two are mutually exclusive by any means—not at all. But most people would measure instinctive success by checking business ledgers, stock investments, annuities, and stock options. Some think that their instinct to increase is about profits and not losses. Many more assume that instinct-based success is about the houses we live in and the cars we drive. They mistake the trinkets of success for success itself.

Others define increase by the score: a home run on a baseball field, or a three-pointer outside the paint on a basketball court. Or it could be celebrities you've met or degrees you've earned or companies you've started. However, a few realize that instincts are more than shrewd investments and buyouts, scoring points or touchdowns.

You see, it's never the money; *it's the confidence you gained while getting it.* It's never the prize; it's what it took to get the prize. It's not the dividend; it's the exhilarating feeling of having invested wisely. In short, my friend, it's not the destination that matters—it's what you see and learn while getting there! It's the investment of your instincts in future growth and success, not just the dividends paid.

Instinct Multiplies Success

While I was reading through the Bible recently, I encountered a story that really drove this home to me. Now, I don't profess to know all that Jesus intended for us to glean from this story I'm about to share. But some of the truths I extracted from the text may help you realize that we are indeed tenders of the soil.

Whether you are Adam in the Garden of Eden or an investor on Wall Street, there's an expectation that you will be responsible enough to take what you've been given and continue to cultivate it and develop it to the best of your ability! Let's consider the lessons in this multilayered masterpiece.

Again, it will be like a man going on a journey, who called his servants and entrusted his wealth to them. To one he gave five bags of gold, to another two bags, and to another one bag, each according to his ability. Then he went on his journey. The man who had received five bags of gold went at once and put his money to work and gained five bags more. So also, the one with two bags of gold gained two more. But the man who had received one bag went off, dug a hole in the ground and hid his master's money.

After a long time the master of those servants returned and settled accounts with them. The man who had received five bags of gold brought the other five. "Master," he said, "you entrusted me with five bags of gold. See, I have gained five more."

His master replied, "Well done, good and faithful servant! You have been faithful with a few things; I will put you in charge of many things. Come and share your master's happiness!"

The man with two bags of gold also came. "Master," he said, "you entrusted me with two bags of gold; see, I have gained two more."

His master replied, "Well done, good and faithful servant! You have been faithful with a few things; I will put you in charge of many things. Come and share your master's happiness!"

Then the man who had received one bag of gold came. "Master," he said, "I knew that you are a hard man, harvesting where you have not sown and gathering where you have not scattered seed. So I was afraid and went out and hid your gold in the ground. See, here is what belongs to you."

His master replied, "You wicked, lazy servant! So you knew that I harvest where I have not sown and gather where I have not scattered seed? Well then, you should have put my money on deposit with the bankers, so that when I returned I would have received it back with interest.

"So take the bag of gold from him and give it to the one who has ten bags. For whoever has will be given more, and they will have an abundance. Whoever does not have, even what they have will be taken from them."

Matthew 25:14–29, NIV

This story wields a powerful punch in showing us how we must seize the opportunities we have been given and have the courage to forge into the unknown. We must facilitate the untapped power of our possibilities and maximize every gift and grace we're given. We must increase the allotment we've been given and leave every situation better than it was before we were entrusted with it.

Imagine how surprised Jesus' disciples must have been to hear such an amazing idea: that a man rich enough to have servants would leave the servants in charge of the wealth! This is an astonishing notion in any society, but it becomes even more impactful when you consider that during Jesus' lifetime people were born into a strict caste system. Most people then usually believed that the affluent were entitled to lead by virtue of their birthright while the less-than must likewise accept their lot in life. The notion of helping others reach a higher station was not popular, not to mention the notion that a master would entrust his goods to his slaves for safekeeping!

For example, consider when the prodigal son tells his father, "Make me as one of thy hired servants" (Luke 15:19). He implies his willingness to be stripped of all rights to inheritance and to occupy a lesser station in life in exchange for the right to come home. Even Jesus himself once said, "The poor you will have with you always" (Mark 14:7). There seems little expectancy beyond benevolence given to the poor. Certainly, there is not a chance to change stations in life or manage investments.

Yet in this story, the wealth has been transferred—at least from a stewardship perspective—from the haves to the have-nots in a graphic and profound way. Not only does the master delegate his wealth, but then he takes his leave! Even with today's much-needed emphasis on equality, I don't know too many people who go on vacation and leave their wealth in the hands of the maid or the gardener!

Why would Jesus suggest such a countercultural, counterintuitive possibility? The master's slaves had no experience with handling business. They had no training with investments or wealth. Why risk it all with someone who has none?

To answer this question, I challenge you to consider how this parable emphasizes the power of instincts and their direct correlation on our status and standards of living.

Relative Rewards

Each servant is given a portion—not equal portions, but all three receive something. One man receives five bags of gold, the second receives two bags of gold, and the third receives one bag. When the master returns, he asks them to account for what they did with what they had. The man with five reports an increase to ten, a 100 percent increase. The next one, who received two, reports that he, too, has doubled his money and now has four.

But the last servant neither increased nor decreased the one bag with which he had been entrusted. The story concludes by making it clear that the master was quite angry at the way this last servant handled what he'd been given! All the others had an increase of 100 percent. I mention this contrast for several reasons.

First, we must realize that whenever we have been given an opportunity, no matter what the arena, we are expected to produce some level of increase. Whether that opportunity is monetary, as it was in the story mentioned above, or whether it is an intangible opportunity, there's an accountability that cannot be ignored.

What are you going to do with what you have been given?

The second item you must consider is that in spite of the fact that no one received the same amount, each was evaluated based on his level of increase. So the excuse that I didn't have what the other guy had is not acceptable. If God holds us to a divine standard, then we're accountable only to the degree we have been gifted.

The third issue lies with the motivation of the servant who had one. His fear of failure compelled him to hide what he'd been given rather than risk it for increase. The thing that leaps at me in his issue is that he hid his talent and exposed his fear. How many of us are doing that in some area of our lives? When, in fact, we should be hiding our fear and exposing our talents!

Finally, the most profound point for me emerges from the fact that the master never asked any of them to increase what they'd been given. While there's no command, it seems apparent that there's a clear expectation to do so. It's inherently understood that it's the servants' responsibility. This unspoken expectation forms the very basis of my main point here. If you're waiting on someone to command you to perform your best and increase your abilities, then you're not in touch with your instincts. If someone has to demand great thinking and intuitive creation from you, it may be that you are not ready to be so honored. Exceeding the requested duties is a sign of instincts well applied!

This kind of instinctive production isn't elicited by the demand of others around us but rather exudes from the creativity within us. New opportunities call us to birth greatness rather than seek shelter in the womb of mediocrity, which offers temporary comfort but cannot sustain our maturation into the fullness of what we were made to be.

The expectation of the master in the story is the same one given to us by God with every new opportunity. It is the chance to harness your ability with your creativity and risk opening the door for promotion to the next level. The next time you are honored with an opportunity, remember that this is your gateway to the next level of living, thinking, and thriving. You are being given more than a chance to succeed—you are given a chance to advance!

I have seen so many people who wasted their lives, their gifts, their money, and all types of opportunities because fear blocked the path to abundance. Like a roadblock on a highway, they seemed unable to get beyond the debris of past accidents in order to find a new route to their success.

We can overcome our fears if we remember that life

does not demand more than what it gives. We can't waste time comparing what we've been given, because we must reserve that energy for unloading to our God-given potential. The gifts may not be in the same dimension or even to the same degree, but that's okay! It may not be on the same level as everyone else's, and that's okay because we're not called to compete with everyone else. We're not called to use others as the barometer of our breakouts. We're called to maximize the fullness of what God has uniquely entrusted to us!

No, we can't afford to allow our neighbor to dictate how we define success. It may not be in the same area, so we are taught not to covet what we've not been allotted. You can hire people to do what you cannot do. There is no time to spend years imitating what we've not been given.

Instead we are asked to measure ourselves by ourselves and to fulfill the unspoken responsibility that comes with the gifts we've been given. Based on this parable, I'm convinced God asks no more and no less from us. There is no expectation or requirement to function on some other guy's level!

The Urgency of Now

However, this unique standard to which God holds us also means that we must accept responsibility for its fulfillment. We don't have to imitate anyone else's success, but we do have to invest our talents in the dreams we've been given.

Unfortunately, there's no instruction manual in the box when you uncrate the gift inside of you. I can't tell you how many times I wished there were some type of specific directions given as to exactly how we should increase the tangible and intangible gifts we have been given in life. The singer has the gift of song but no sheet music revealing whether to teach, perform, or record. The artist has the gift of drawing, but there is no clear blueprint as to whether he should pursue graphic design or fine art landscapes.

In fact, if instructions were included with our gifts, then our instincts would not have to be activated. God doesn't give details when he gives gifts. He just gives us the instinct and the opportunity. He allows us to meet the right people at the right time and challenge us with how they perceive our capacity to perform. When life gives us gifts and an opportunity to use those gifts, this in itself is a compliment and, more important, our permission to advance.

So don't wait on someone else to tell you how, when, and where to do what only you can know inside you. No one will tell you this is the moment. No announcer will declare this is the opportunity you've been waiting for. No parent, spouse, business partner, mentor, lover, coach, teacher, or pastor can tell you the time of your appointment with destiny.

Instead there is only an instinct of urgency. There is

an instinct of necessity. There is a still, small voice that says, "To him whom much is given much is required." There is this moment *right now*!

I've often had people write me on Facebook or Twitter and ask, "How do I know what I'm created to do?" When these pop up, I have a habit of looking at the profile of the people who question. More times than not, I am expecting a college student or a high school sophomore to be the one asking such questions. But that's not always the case—or even usually the case.

Many times people in their forties and fifties are still standing over the box of life trying to find the directions as to how they should put together what they have been given. Many spend their entire lives at the crossroads of greatness trying to decipher which way they should go. They do not know that the longer they deliberate the more they lose. The singer loses his voice with age. The runner's legs get stiff as time passes her by. The business environment changes with the ebbing and flowing of the economy. Lost time means irretrievably lost opportunities.

During his campaigns, President Barack Obama used a phrase from Dr. Martin Luther, "the fierce urgency of now." This alarm-clock quotation reminds all of us that time's loss is something no one can afford. Just as the master's servants were required to think like a master despite their status as slaves, we must seize the moments we're given to be more than our circumstances dictate.

At the end of the day, the slaves' station in life rose—or sank—to the level of their thinking. These individuals used what they had in a timely way and thereby, in spite of the societal laws of the times, moved into the dimension of their master. Despite their station in life, they thought beyond where they were and moved in the direction of where they wanted to go.

Consider another example. In the dark history of the formation of our country, the enslaved were forbidden to learn how to read. The slave owners of that time understood all too well: the key to freedom was in the mind of the enslaved. Once the person in bondage thought like a free being, they would be nearly impossible to control. If you liberate someone's thinking, it is only a matter of time before chains cannot hold their liberated mentality.

That is why I never allow people to incarcerate my thinking by forcing their opinion on me. I always listen in case I can gain some wisdom that influences me. But when they try to berate me and disrespect me with the force of their ideas, the conversation is always over.

Why? Because my thinking epitomizes my freedom. Whenever you give someone the deed of trust over your mind, they have in fact become your master. The Bible says it this way, "As a man thinketh, so is he" (Prov. 23:7). How you think about your opportunities determines how you will act on them.

Threshold of Success

Finally, we must notice that the master's final com-mendation to his wise and faithful servants is an invitation, "Come and share your master's happi-ness!" This is in fact the crossover moment beyond the parameters of where you started. The servants had shattered the glass ceiling and had a chance, in spite of the normative constraints of the time, to advance to the next dimension of living.

They could now enter into the joy of a change in sta-tus. Enter into the freedom that comes with a change in responsibility. Enter into a rebranding of who they were and how they lived. Simply put, this is how peo-ple excel. They do so by maintaining a commitment to underpromise and overdeliver.

Not one of the servants took his initial opportu-nity and started bragging about what he could do. He simply did what was in him to do. In return, the "well done" they received wasn't based on a quota. One returned with ten and the other with four. But each performed 100 percent at his level. This is so vitally important that I'll say it again: you aren't in a race with a level of gifting that is beyond what you were given. The promotion is based on what you did with what *you* had! The result of your authentic stewardship is always promotion.

The knocking of opportunity, if answered in this way, will inevitably result with promotion into the next dimension. Can you imagine how the other servants perceived these stewards when they went back to their slave quarters and started shoving their meager personal effects into a bag? Their peers might have asked, "Where are you going?" And the response would've been, "We're moving into the master's quarters—not as servants but as masters." Such a moment would be too surreal to describe, too magical to articulate. The intoxicating feeling of promotion is the entrance to the new opportunities of the next dimension.

You yourself are on the cusp of such a transition. Have you ever experienced this kind of growth before? Think back; I'm sure you have. It's the kind of promotion that makes you drive home from work giggling to yourself in the car! It's the kind of advancement that brings joyful exuberance and confidence, because you know you've done what only you can do—you've given it your all and been recognized for it! This kind of exhilaration causes the soul to soar. These moments may include financial advancement, but tangible assets are not the greatest reward.

The greatest reward is the confirmation of what you already knew instinctively. You've received an answer to the haunting, alluring question forever dancing around the edges of your mind. "Yes—you were made for more!" your reward proclaims. It is the answer to the question that most of us have within regarding our greater call, our greater purpose, and some greater expectation beyond our circumstance.

The voice inside was right! The inclinations were true. My instinct was accurate. What started out as a suspicion, a hypothesis, an intuition, has now evolved into sheer confirmation. It changes the deepest part of how we see ourselves and culminates in a transformation of how others perceive us as well.

My hope is that these truths may be the tutoring you need to prepare you for activating your instinct to increase. It's time for you to respond to the rapping fist of opportunity's fierce knock on the door of your life right now. If you will answer the knock and honor the chance with discipline, creativity, and urgency, you may find yourself—your true self—living a life that exceeds your wildest dreams!

CHAPTER 12

⊞◇⊞

Protection from Predators

Ihave a pair of Roman Cane Corso dogs named Bentley and Sable, male and female respectively. If you aren't familiar with the breed, their strength is similar to the pit bull's but they have a much different personality. Highly intelligent and excellent workers, these dogs descended from ancient Italy, where they often fought wild predators. A few years ago, my wife gave them to me as a Christmas gift as she knows that I'm intrigued by animals and their calming effect.

After my dogs arrived and got old enough to roam our property, they discovered the primal playmates lurking nearby: squirrels along with an occasional bobcat and a coyote or two. Yes, in Texas you can't always see the native inhabitants until they want you to see them! I enjoyed watching my new pets settle into their new environment with so much to figure out. Even seemingly simple decisions like where to mark their territory and where to hide their toys fascinated me. Since I can't communicate in their language, we had to figure out each other's expectations as they adjusted to the other animals who predated their arrival.

They love my backyard, with its ample room to roll around and frolic. They wrestle with each other and play chase. They run after the squirrels and bark at them, other times chasing a wild rabbit. Their presence makes me smile, and their affection fills a void in a way I can't explain. They bring out the little boy in me I thought was long gone. In some ways my dogs resurrect that child and give him a place to express himself. In exchange, I give them food and shelter, safety, and great medical care. I keep them clean and their coats brushed.

No matter how beautiful they look and how well-behaved they act, sometimes at night I hear them growl and snarl. Then I'm reminded that their basic instincts always guide them. Bentley and Sable know that everyone out there isn't as happy to see them as I am. In those moments I realize that loving them and brushing them, feeding them and scratching their bellies, can never subdue their natural proclivities. When my backyard turns into a nighttime jungle, their claim on the territory has to be defended.

A few times I've had to bandage some wounds from

my dogs' fights that went on without my knowledge. Love them all I want, I can't save them from the system of induction to the elements that preceded their arrival. Maybe Bentley and Sable were surprised by some nocturnal predator, but more than likely they smelled his scent and anticipated his attack. They instinctively know what they must do to protect themselves from predators.

Prey for Your Predators

When we enter a new environment, we must prepare ourselves for the same kind of adversity. Sometimes the splendor, the challenge, and the brilliance of affirmation shine so brightly that those who are blessed to step into a new jungle become dazzled by the opportunity and blinded to the adversity. No matter how friendly the welcome party seems, always know that the bobcats come out at night!

Whenever you arrive on the shores of a new career, vocation, or aspiration, you always arrive as an immigrant. You have a different scent on you, and all the animals know it! What looks like a backyard when you step into it will always have eyes glaring in the shadows, and native noses in the air catching the scent of the outsider who now has changed the balance in the backyard. No amount of kindness can alter the fact that the other animals in your new world feel threatened by your arrival—which means you must be prepared to do some sniffing as well!

Fools rush in where the brave dare not tread. And while it is a wonderful blessing to have the gate open to a fresh opportunity, it is naïve to think that you are walking into a sterile, unbiased environment. So sniff out your new world before you do too much barking. Knowing who's who will save you from ending up on the menu of some overly aggressive, attention-starved, attack-prone coyote who comes out only at night.

In other words, nothing takes the place of research when you are in a new environment. Most businesses fail because their founders' decisions were not preceded with adequate due diligence. Marriages often fail because dating didn't sniff the ground where old bones might be buried. Churches often crumble when pastors don't engage the neighborhood but choose to isolate their flock when instead they need to integrate with the environment in which they reside.

Most newbies come in making too much noise to notice the eyes that stare behind the smiles that quickly fade. They enter into conversations when they should be nodding, smiling, and listening. In new environments, you must learn to read the body language as well as the new words in the native tongue. So much can be communicated that's contrary to what is actually being said.

New dogs in the yard don't usually know the rules

of engagement. It is most important that you do a lot of looking and sniffing before you do much barking. Others already know you are there. Proceed with caution without looking afraid.

If a new world just opened up for you, always remember that you are the immigrant no matter how well you appear to fit in. And more times than not, immigrants have a hard time migrating into new worlds without conflict. Your degree may prepare you to perform the task. Your experience and creativity might show you how to enhance the property. But if your instincts don't tell you what's around you, you're bound to get bitten!

Instinctive Behavior

The animalistic instinct we were equipped with as part of the survival mechanisms God gave us are often underutilized. We must remember that due diligence and responsible research exceed magazines and books, manuals and procedures. New jungles always maintain specific codes of conduct that only can be sniffed out once you're in the midst of the wilderness.

Whether your new arena is as benign as church or as jaundiced as politics, do not be deceived: all backyards are jungles. And though you have new horizons and deep aspirations, do not become so intoxicated with what this means to you that you fail to assess what your arrival means to them. So as you survey the land and familiarize yourself with the topography of the new arena, don't forget to keep your nose to the wind! Because in the world of new conquest, instincts are king!

No matter how big their smiles and how flattering their speeches, every jungle has its predators. Every job has its gangs and gang leaders. It won't be typed on their ID badges as you meet them at the office potluck or spelled out on their name tags during the team-building exercise, so don't bother looking there. Nonetheless, tigers have their stripes and gang members have their colors, which may not be apparent to you at first glance.

So take your time and get your bearings. See how you can communicate effectively and interact with each different species rather than automatically making enemies with one because of aligning yourself with another. Don't rush into alliances without thinking through the implications.

I've always avoided being quick to take sides. As I entered into the public arena because of my ministry, I often found myself alongside politicians and other stakeholders who didn't always see my arrival as auspicious. Instead of perceiving our vessel as a cruise ship embarking happy tourists, they often viewed us as soldiers infiltrating their shores from a battleship! But regardless of how we were greeted, my response to new environments has always remained the same—avoid taking sides in battles that started before you even showed up!

Ofield Dukes, the late legendary public relations pioneer, did some work for me in the early years of my career. When he asked about my politics, I told him, "I'm nonpartisan and plan to stay that way." Inexperienced in the new worlds where I found myself, my response reflected my attempt at avoiding allegiance in these new spheres that seemed as different from mine as the south side of the North Pole!

Of course, I had political opinions but I kept them to myself. Even then I knew labels can be libelous when you're immigrating to the next level of living. Any side you choose will inherently create enemies of the rival gang. I also recognized that even those with similar sensibilities may see your shared colors not as a new alliance but as a threat to their position. If you don't watch those who claim to have your back, you'll eventually find yourself lying on it!

Now, *nonpartisan* was not a term Ofield Dukes was used to hearing from the mouth of a black clergyman. At that time it was a forgone conclusion that if you were a black preacher you could sing well, eat your weight in fried chicken, and schmooze with the Democratic Party. So he was stunned to hear that I wore no uniform for either team.

In response, however, he said something to me that I've never forgotten. Looking me in the eye, he warned,

"He who walks in the middle of the road gets hit by both sides!" Little did I know that his words would be so prophetic.

I have been hit like a football quarterback, bruised like the knees of a little boy with a new bike, and bitten like a dog that woke a coyote sleeping in his yard! Yet for the life of me, I still think you must avoid latching onto a label while you're still reeling from disorientation. After all, I was the new kid on the block, with no aspirations to run for office. I wasn't there for the politics, but I sure found out that politicians would be there for me! The good, the bad, and the ugly all come out to meet you when you are a new inductee. Some will come to recruit you. Others will come out to inspect you. And a few will come to exterminate you! Your instincts may not be able to prevent some of these blows, but they can help you protect yourself and minimize their impact.

Your Instinctive Identity

So what do you do when these attempts lead to an attack? How do you survive and thrive in your destiny without becoming a blink in history? Once again, I learned from Bentley and Sable, my hairy, slobbering friends. Their unique qualities have taught me to use who you are to adapt to where you find yourself.

You see, as canines, they can't connect with the rabbits nor are they designed to. They can't climb trees with the squirrels, or hide under roots like the chipmunks. They may resemble the coyotes, but they aren't one of them. Perhaps that's why it's good that they have each other. The shared experience of frolicking like pets in the day and fighting like soldiers at night bonds them together.

And they also share the love, attention, and sustenance offered by their owner. For you see, no matter what happens in the suburban jungles of night, whether they return with birds in their mouths or blood on their torsos, they always come back to their home base. They know who they are, whose they are, and ultimately where they belong.

The same is true for you! Many people will want to use your mouth to convey their message. Don't let them. Others will try to harness your influence for their agenda. Resist them. There will be moments when someone steals your thunder, mauls your paws, and nips your nose. But you can always survive the treacheries and tragedies if you have a base to which you can return. Never allow the other animals to overwhelm you so much that you lose your way back to where you belong. Always know your base, that calm core of confidence within you, and how to access it and take shelter as needed.

You must be true to your purpose, doggedly tenacious

about your passion, and never lose sight of your center. You can't be balanced without a center point upon which other forces tilt. That part that doesn't move within you controls all that is moving around you. If you lose your center and forgo your identity, then you're done, finished, kaput!

Whether you win or lose today's skirmish for survival doesn't matter as much as maintaining your base. I've seen my dogs come back to the house with possums in their mouths, wagging their tails with glee. I've also seen them come back with blood running down their legs with lacerations from a bobcat as their only reward. But they always come back to the base.

If you lose your sense of who you are, you have nothing to which you can return. If you don't discover your passions, purpose, and power, then you will pursue the roles assigned by other people's scripts. You will lose the success afforded by new opportunities if you don't know your own priorities and preferences.

Your strength is in your uniqueness. If you lose yourself just to get along with others, then you have nothing original to offer this new world of possibilities. In spy language, you have been compromised. In scientific language, you have been neutralized. In corporate language, you have become redundant. In short, you become liquidated, excommunicated, and eradicated!

Stay true to yourself while you integrate what you

have into where you are. Chase the squirrels, fight the bobcats, and roll in the grass, but hold on to what makes you just as unique as my Roman Cane Corsos. Whether you're in victory or agony, you will always survive to fight another day if you refuse to compromise and make your instinctive calling your compass!

CHAPTER 13

Informed Instincts

Relying on your instincts is not enough. You might survive but you won't thrive without due diligence and the research needed to sharpen and hone your instincts. I'm convinced instincts operate most accurately when they have as much data as possible. Our instincts then process the facts, figures, and financials through the filters of our personalities, experiences, and goals. It's where art and science meet to create this most unique navigational system for living.

As we learn to live by instinct, we will draw on all we've experienced: all our tests and tragedies, triumphs and setbacks. Curiously enough, the word *science* is derived from the Latin word *scientia*, which at its core means "knowledge." And knowledge comes in part from experiences and in part from encounters.

Every systematic enterprise must build and organize

acquired knowledge in the form of testable hypotheses and calculated predictions about its environment. As surely as my backyard turned into a jungle at night for my dogs, your new level of achievement will become your laboratory for innovation and improvisation. Before making assumptions based on prior knowledge, compare what you've learned to what you observe around you. If you study your strides, you're less likely to stumble!

Get Your Bearings

While it's wonderful to know what you know, wisdom requires that you also know what you don't know without getting the two confused. There's much to be learned about where you are and how what you know fits into what you do not know. When the technician ascends to management, she must quickly recognize that people require more than mechanisms. When the employee becomes the employer, he must resist hiring and firing based on where he used to be instead of where he is.

I shared in the last chapter how I've tried to avoid becoming partisan in a politically charged situation. Several years ago during an election year, I was invited to the Christian Coalition of America because I was an up-and-coming minister whose biblical views might have made me a good prospect for the right wing. And that same year I was asked to speak at the Rainbow Coalition! Its members recognized that there were many issues that the coalition cared about that deeply concerned me also.

Both groups had invited me in part because of my growth in ministry and my arrival on the shores of this new world of public policy and political activism. As I went to both meetings and listened and watched and sniffed and prayed, I knew that I had stumbled into a big field of ideas and dangers, secrets and sciences, that I would spend the next few years trying to untangle. And in the midst of all the push-pulling of my new peers, the operative question in my mind reflected the query of any new immigrant: where do I fit, if at all, in this new and exciting world?

Now, you might say, "I'm not Bishop Jakes and I don't have those issues to balance and sort through." But before you draw this conclusion, think again. Whether you're a new hire, a new business owner, a new partner in the club, a new investor in the firm, or a newlywed, this applies to you. If you're a new alto in the choir or a new council member in the city, you have stepped into a field filled with fire and folly. Don't think for one minute that you can pretend to be unaffected by the forces flying at you from every direction!

Don't assume that you can rely on your instincts for information that's easily accessible in other ways. In other words, know the facts before you reflect on your feelings. Do the work necessary to be up to speed and informed about all angles of a problem, conflict, or issue.

I would like to think that I've been able to serve presidents and other political leaders in both major parties because of my ability to understand where they're each coming from. Although I may not agree with certain stands, statutes, or strategies, I try to respect others by seeing things through their eyes.

In other words, your instincts need to know the boundaries before they can help you get your bearings. Just as animals mark their territory so that they will recognize it later, we need to know the lay of the land before we begin traipsing through it. Is that the North Star or a train coming toward us? Is this snowball going to roll until it causes an avalanche or will it melt at our feet? Without tending to the basics of investigation and research, it's impossible for our instincts to guide us accurately.

Heightened Instincts

Now, you can read the employee manual, or Google the data on your new venture. You can gather the statistics and memorize the demographics in your mind. But the truth remains that in each new jungle you enter, an unwritten code of conduct guides its inhabitants. Each world has a host of special interest groups, causes to join, fraternities and sororities, and secret societies. These various groups will be blazing trails to mark their territory while you're still using GPS to get across the street!

Remember that while you're the immigrant learning the lingo, everyone else is native to the process. So before you take a nap under a tree, or make camp in a clearing, you better sniff around the bushes and discern what else is lurking around you.

There are ways to get things done that aren't recorded. There are ways to inherit enemies, encounter bullies, and sabotage your success that you haven't even thought about. And there are thousands of predators right in your own backyard who don't come out till the sun goes down. You might not see these night stalkers, but wherever you go, the gang's always there!

Balancing who you are with where you are is another science all to itself. On one hand, if you do not define yourself, your enemies will try to define you. So you have to be busy in the business of branding. But while you're trying to get the right message out about who you are, you must also learn to locate yourself within the context of currents swirling around you. Variable conditions, allegiances, and allies shift frequently. If it weren't enough to adjust to the new world to which you're acclimating, you must also become adept at negotiating negatives and leveraging positives about what you came to do.

You'll barely have time to unpack your bags in Bugtussle, USA, before you're dancing with danger and waltzing with wolves. Strangely enough, your accomplishment cannot fully be celebrated before it's time to decamp, defend, and debrief. Whenever you're thrust into the wild, someone or something will immediately pick up your scent and make strategic decisions regarding their response to your arrival.

The agendas are endless, the enemies everywhere, and the allies often apathetic. Fan clubs and fight clubs all meet on the same street corner. The difference between a friend and a foe can be as subtle as the distinction between identical twins. That is to say, you can scarcely tell them apart! Anyone who has ever taken a position at a new company, or married a pastor, or moved into a new neighborhood, ought to give me a good amen!

Finding Where You Belong

If you don't find a way to enhance your instinct through research, you forfeit the opportunity to belong. I've had to let many people go from my company and occasionally from my church staff. It wasn't always an indication that the person wasn't good at what they do. Many times the problem arose from their inability to acclimate to their new environment. They could do the task but could not socially and professionally adapt to new ways of interaction, communication, and delegation. It doesn't matter how good you are at what you do if you can't fit into your new environment.

It's a science, so study it. It's a laboratory experiment to discover what you can and cannot say. It's listening to your instincts as well as the insinuations of your new associates. And learning in the lab remains dangerous, since not all chemicals mix well! Chemical reactions can produce powerful results that either destroy or create energy for the organization.

And keep in mind that scientists must get outside their laboratories. Like zoologists in the jungle, you must learn to study the creatures with whom you cohabit. You must dwell among them, but you can't be one of them. They'll let you know that you live on the same street but you might not be a part of the gang. Learning to survive with the gangs without wearing their colors to work is a tricky business. It is a process and, God knows, it is a science.

You'll realize fairly quickly that most species tend to stick together. The rabbits may scamper like squirrels, but they don't play with them. The coyotes are strong and quick, hungry and ruthless. They've learned how to join forces in a pack without inviting the bobcats or the jackals. Record the habits of those in your new jungle, but don't allow yourself to follow the same patterns unless you're making a deliberate choice.

Study Your Own Habits

The challenge is to accomplish your assignment without losing your identity. Your presence changes the ecosystem and alters the environment for better and/ or for worse. In the process of adjustments there will be conflicts. There will always be those moments where principles you used in your former life disappoint you in your current environment. This lesson is fundamental. You can't take everything you used before with you. Your ability to survive has everything to do with your ability to adapt.

Adapting and surviving requires that you know your own proclivities and preferences, your default settings and disciplines. You must protect your soft areas and use your strengths to provide cover. Increasing the power of your instincts means learning more about yourself than ever before.

Like all sciences, there will be failed experiments and lost investments. But these will teach you something—if nothing else, through the power of elimination—if you're willing to proceed patiently. The loss of time, effort, and dollars becomes the price to be paid when your ultimate objective is to accelerate and not just acclimate. When you want to reach solid conclusions and not tentative theories, then you must be willing to risk what you know for what you want to know.

Inform your instincts and you'll improve your potency, no matter what jungle you find yourself in!

CHAPTER 14

— ⬦ —

Instinctive Leadership

We instinctively know how to lead if we allow ourselves.

While no two leaders are exactly the same and each will vary their style and method, all individuals leading by instinct explore the distance between where they've been and where they're going. Some approach leadership based on their strength or the strength of the team, others on their previous organization's culture or the culture that was established when they got there. They inherit systems and struggles that in no way resemble the vision and mandate that they are most passionate about. They must then decide: who stays and who goes?

At my core I am a motivator, and I love to invest in people. The question for me was centered around people resources. Can I develop what I have, or should I look outside of my organization for what I need? This dilemma has led to inner turmoil many times as my heart said "Let them stay" when my head said "Let them go!"

You see, I have spent years as a pastor where the goal is retention. Spiritual leaders are often evaluated on their ability to sustain momentum, maintain the budget, and retain the membership. All of that works well if you are involved only with members or, perhaps in your case, customers or clients. But most businesses, as well as the enterprise of pursuing our God-given destinies, require more than just customer service. There has to be a team approach to unite the various departments required for success, whether those are human resources and internal technology or your personal resources and your laptop. The big question remains: how do I retain what I need and release what I do not?

I had to learn as my staff increased that my model of leadership needed a serious overhaul. The same proclivities that made me an effective pastor did not necessarily produce the skill set required for greater leadership of my business team and personal staff. But I learned that from the moment a pastor employs people, his propensity to shepherd a flock can come back to bite him.

In short, your gifting and opportunity can bring you into a new arena that your skill sets may be able to manage but not maximize. With these new opportunities, your mentality is influenced not by where you're going but more aptly by where you've been. But surely you see the danger in such an approach. A new suit doesn't change the old man! A new hairdo won't transform the woman beneath the bangs!

You can't function on the next level if you still have the old style of leadership. Many people move into a new opportunity, but they have the past mentality and soon they find that they are having experiences that poison the fresh chance with old contaminates. You can't revamp a department if you yourself carry the methodology of where you were and not where you are!

As my business involvement beyond the pulpit grew, so did my struggles to lead in these new endeavors. Suddenly I was hiring staff, maintaining a for-profit entity, and developing people around new goals. Unfortunately, while I had the corporate structure of a business for my enterprise, I still had pastoral tendencies. I had to learn to distinguish ministry from management and potlucks from portfolios. The Sunday school classroom is not the boardroom!

You can't reform the organization if its leader communicates old messages and ideas by virtue of language and habits from the past. A new logo is nice, a new brand is wonderful, but if the old culture persists you are destined for self-sabotage!

Tradition vs. Innovation

I found myself in meetings with high-level CEOs one moment and strong pastoral leaders the next. While there are many similarities between business and pastoral leaders, there are also many differences. I struggled with the models of my friends, who were sacred leaders functioning largely with a pastoral focus not only with the flock but also with the team. They, more times than not, lacked the fortitude to make the decisions that needed to be made for their organizations to thrive. They often chose the retention model: catch all you can. Often they were not leading by instinct but by tradition. They kept the peace and maintained the status quo but later became frustrated as the church suffered from their indecisive leadership. It was withering not because of lack of vision but because there was a serious disconnect between the leader and those who represented him.

Often the ministry doesn't flourish because the leader lacks the ability to prune the vine they worked all their lives to grow! Instead of growing in productivity, it is really the same old things from days gone by. The soil never rests and new seeds are never planted. The harvest still yields fruit, but it's proportionately less with each passing season. This is not growth; it is simply swelling, with the infection of the past world mixed with the new opportunity!

But the antithesis of this, based on what I witnessed from my associates in the business world, is the release model. Their idea is to be slow to hire and quick to fire. Sudden turnovers, they say, are the nature of the beast. My corporate friends believe that releasing should always be quick and definitive. They choose change at any cost, often overriding the wisdom of their instincts for stability.

However, sometimes retention is a good thing. Developing and training those who have been loyal can create a sense of family that's very important to the well-being of the whole organization. If team members do not feel secure and invested, they will not commit their personal gifts toward full productivity for the organization.

The recent recession we faced in our nation and all the layoffs that ensued showed us that when people are uncertain of what will happen next, they withdraw to "wait and see." Spending shuts down, anxiety mounts, divorces increase, and productivity is compromised as team members develop an "every man for himself" stance. Many people are traumatized by uncertainty. It is the silent killer of relationships at work and at home. Anytime people don't know where they stand, they either leave physically and/or detach emotionally. Either way, when you're paralyzed by fear of the unknown, it doesn't matter which direction you're headed because you're not moving!

Similarly, when you operate based on a formula or a one-size-fits-all model, you miss the power and insight your instincts can bring. Tradition and innovation must work in harmony for maximum success, and our instincts know how to maintain this equilibrium. Based on specific data, context, and timing, instinct can become a leader's greatest tool for knowing when to stay the course and when to change direction.

Contagious Instincts

Honing your instinct for creative change at the right time sharpens the instincts of those around you. In this regard, leading by instinct can become contagious. If the people you retain don't respond to that retention and reward it with an earnest effort to remain relevant, then it backfires. The onus rests upon the team to avail themselves of all available opportunities supplied to stay cutting-edge. While the company can identify training, the persons who are a part of the team share some serious responsibility not to become inflexible or irrelevant by virtue of thinking that a good relationship and personality will cover a poor performance.

If such complacency develops, the organization will suffer from paralysis and lose its sense of direction. This is also true in the home. Both parties have to maintain vigilance to be progressive and innovative. Just because people stay married doesn't mean that they are happily married. In that same sense, just because you've been with a task a long time doesn't mean that you have remained relevant. It is wise to stay abreast of the latest information that will cause you to be able to grow forward and not just go forward. An ancient book of wisdom tells us "Iron sharpens iron," and indeed it does.

But rust also results in rust! If the team atmosphere becomes strained, the vitality dissipates and gradually toxicity ensues. So if the stagnancy is not eradicated, then growth is compromised and other good people gradually move on. It's hard to gain speed in the present, let alone map future destinations, when certain tires are stuck in reverse!

Removing the bottleneck that is the stagnant staff member or leader is also appreciated, because truly creative people actually feel like they are asphyxiating when they are placed beneath someone whose only contribution to a meeting is "that's not how we used to do it." I can't tell you how many homes, churches, and businesses are engaged in a civil war, because they don't have a sincere appreciation for the individuals. They are at war between what *was* and what *is*.

Whenever *what was* begins to fight against *what is*, they both jeopardize the future of *what can be*! The damage will be collateral and the impact will be comprehensive.

When Instincts Are Ignored

Now, just because an idea is new doesn't mean that it's progressive. And when new ideas are seriously evaluated and considered before being dismissed, those who present them feel affirmed. But when those ideas have no more chance of consideration than a snowman in hell, the instinct for creativity is dwarfed by the toxic cultural work environment! So you may have succeeded in appeasing the vanguards of the organization, but you do so at the expense of retarding the growth of what you had hoped to build.

So then if you are in touch with the pulse of the team you are leading, you notice the new creative life ebb from new inductees in the firm. Additionally, those who have been long-term veterans of the organization are stuck, and the paralysis immobilizes relevance. Gradually you will notice people who were once excited move on—or worse, they remain on the team with nothing in view but pensions or personal gain. They will channel their creativity into personal ventures or mislabel line items on your budget sheet as costs that are actually a deep waste, so you get little to no return on your investment!

These dynamics create an apathy throughout the entire organization, a slow paralysis of which few will even speak openly. This paralysis may not start out flaunting itself on a ledger sheet. That is to say, there's more to running an organization than numbers. It may not initially show itself in the death of dollars; rather, it shows in the slow, agonizing death of new ideas.

It begins like a silent cancer waiting to metastasize throughout the corporate body. When new and creative ideas stop coming in, energy dissipates and morale declines. When team members do not experience instinctive leadership, they retreat to safe models that ensure job security even as their retreat ironically threatens the health of the entire organization. There's no immunity to fight the growing dis-ease. Eventually, lower profits will reflect that the infection has spread to the balance sheet, and the economics will be a symptom and not a source of the deeper problem.

Without an infusion of instinct and an elevation of its importance in the company or team, eventually productivity dries up and the stream of innovation trickles to a stop. Instinct is that important to how you lead. When instincts are ignored, leaders become followers, and followers become unemployed!

Builders and Bankers

Many leaders fall into one of two categories, while instinct-led leaders know both areas are required for healthy growth and advancement. Builders are those people who are motivated by challenge. They have to have something to build, something to fight, or something that gives them quantifiable results. These people are designed to keep the entity vibrant. They are sometimes spontaneous, always creative, and perpetually most engaged when there is action.

And then there are bankers. Bankers are like country

wood-burning stoves. They feel a sense of achievement from maintenance. They like to sustain and maintain what someone else built. These people are great at the critical systems that need to be put into place to make sure that we aren't always building without banking enough wood for the next fire and the long winter ahead. Builders make money; bankers save it. Builders keep the marriage exciting; bankers keep the home grounded. Builders can draw a crowd; bankers can train the crowd that's gathered.

Both are required for the growth of a healthy company, relationship, or endeavor. The dynamic, productive tension between them works beautifully until you put a banker in charge of project development or a new business acquisition! The bankers can't lead because they only want to keep it like it was originally. The builder who needs fresh incentive is stuck in gridlock on a highway of unrealized opportunity. And the lion and the lamb lie down together in a nightmare of frustration. So you're left looking at a quarterly report humming Marvin Gaye's hit song from the seventies, "What's Going On."

It isn't just about having the right people in your life. It's also about location, location, location. We've cut away the hemorrhaging resources from wasted energy and income on those who refuse to grow. We have retained the best and brightest, keeping them challenged and innovative. Like spark plugs in the engine, everyone is in place and this thing begins to lurch forward. Those fueled by instinct know how to maximize their engine's horsepower by building it from the very best components.

As you explore all your leadership opportunities—not just the ones at the office—make sure your vehicle has what it takes to navigate the jungles ahead. Once you allow your instinct to fuel your engine, you're ready to maximize your leadership potential and locate the elephants just around the corner. So take your foot off the brake, ease off the clutch, and let's shift into the next gear of your instinct-led adventure.

Independent Yet Ineffective

When we harness the synthesis of wisdom from our instincts with ongoing education, instinctive leadership grows stronger and stronger. Instinctive leadership grows from seeds of responsibility and influence.

I recognized this fruitful combination in my oldest son by the way he held his bottle when he was in his crib. I remember so well watching him taking the bottle—quite prematurely, I might add—from his mother. People were amazed at his independence at such an early age. He was only a few months old and he was already holding his bottle like he was a grown man. He was self-contained and has always been rather independent.

Now, to be sure, many years later this characteristic

often caused him to be selected to lock up the house or park the car. But the downside was that it left him without the doting attention many children get. I've noticed, even in responding to children, people don't support independent individuals with the same gravitas they do those who expose their dependency and vulnerability.

And such was the case with my oldest child. He didn't need as much help getting dressed, or getting in the car, or completing homework, because he showed us that he could do it without us. Instinctively, he gravitated to roles of independence, which is a good thing experientially but can be debilitating emotionally. While independence may signal the genesis of leadership, it is far from the completion of it.

Leadership emerges not only when an individual can capably do what needs doing; the real test is passed when a person can implement what needs to be done through others. If you want to lead by your instincts, then you must ask yourself: can you inspire those who work around you to join your efforts?

Leading by instinct requires you to influence others as you amass a pool of support. If you are to achieve the dreams set before you, it will require a team effort, with many supporting players. Your instincts can help you assemble the best team and retain these talented individuals, but you must also be able to influence them. Knowing what motivates them to new heights is part of this instinctive influence. Managing conflict, creating innovative solutions, and maintaining your strength of character and moral center also influences others.

People instinctively want to trust the leader they follow. They want to believe he or she is worthy of their investment of time and effort. They want to know that their leaders will recognize their value and enhance their skill set. Instinctive leaders know that if they cannot influence those around them, then their boundaries shrink. You can't produce as much product, distribute it, maintain it, and extend in new directions without influencing others. Your capital is also limited without the ability to influence others.

If you rely only on yourself, then your income is limited by you being your only resource. If you want to be a great doctor, then practice medicine. But if you want to be wealthy, successful, and expand your ability to bring healing to your community, then open up an office and hire several doctors. In the pursuit of hands-on businesses, always know that there will be a salary cap. The cap comes as you realize that no matter how fruitful you may be, you remain limited unless you can reduplicate your capabilities and extend your vision to others.

If you lead by instinct, then you will know your

priorities. Increasing the size of your business, influence, and income may not be as important as protecting your privacy, maintaining stability, and enjoying ample leisure time. You instinctively know what you want, so don't lead yourself and others to someone else's destination. You may prize independence over innovation. However, if your natural instinct for independence remains unchecked, you may not mature.

Independent leaders may be surrounded by people but refuse to use their influence as well as to be influenced by their team members. In fact, people typically don't assist independent leaders because they look like they can handle it all alone. If you send the signal that you don't need help, then others will receive it accordingly.

While I applaud that you can do it alone, always remember that if you can do a task, you will always have a job. But if you know why the task must be tackled, then you can delegate others to work for you! The why and the when of a task is inclusive of leadership instincts. While the how-to-do-it will always lead to a job, if you want more than just a job, you must know the why and when of a thing and not just the how.

Instinctive Risks

While instinctive leaders know they must balance independence with influence, they must also balance risk with responsibility. It can be frightening to move from a one-person pursuit of a dream to a team approach. When I hired my first administrative assistant, I was deathly afraid of being responsible for her salary and benefits. I took comfort in the fact that her husband had a good-paying job, so if my enterprise failed, then she would not go hungry or lose her home.

However, a short time later, I needed to expand the vision and take another risk toward fulfilling my destiny. I hired a man who gave up his job to come and work for me, and I was burdened by the weight of feeling responsible for his success as well as my own. While it was tempting to try and be Superman for everyone I hired, ultimately, I realized that they were aware of the risks and nonetheless wanted to be part of something bigger.

Independent leaders also discover the emotional toll of their self-sufficiency even after they have assembled a team and delegated their responsibilities. Since they are often denied help when others logically assume they don't need it, they keep assuming it's all up to them alone. Independent leaders sometimes have to overcome the instinct to be a lone wolf and instead lead the pack.

When you operate independently in the midst of your team, it stunts their growth as well as your own. You don't want to lead a task, run a business, direct a philanthropy, or guide a church if your stakeholders assume you don't need their help. If you want to lead by your instincts, then you must create a vision large enough that you cannot achieve it alone. You want something so much bigger than you that you must delegate to a team.

Interdependence is the real indicator that a strong leader is emerging. Anything you can lead alone isn't much. You want something that is so far beyond your own capabilities that it will require a task force to achieve the goal. So don't pick something your own size. Make the garment of your dreams big enough for the child of your labors to grow into it.

If you have the courage to take on a project that requires assistance, other gifted people will become invested in your cause. I've found that people are much more willing to galvanize around a mission and not just the man. Inspirational leaders ignite a spark within us that compels us to be part of the blaze they are lighting. When you inspire people to come on board with you, you are evolving into an instinctive leader.

Instinctive Leaders Lead

Do you remember the 2008 Democratic primaries when then Senator Hillary Clinton was running against then Senator Barack Obama? It was certainly a memorable race. The ratings on the networks were sky-high and the entire world was watching as our nation conducted an ongoing conversation about who should hold the Oval Office. Frequently, some pundit or commentator asked: when the phone rings at three in the morning, which candidate would be most adept at answering that call? Which would answer and provide us with the security of their leadership?

We know the results of that race, but election time is not the only season when we must assess our instinctive leadership qualities. Life continuously makes a call for leadership. This call is often a cause, ringing through a problem, need, or conflict. Others say, "Someone should do something," while leaders are already doing it. Leaders may have fears or uncertainties, but they instinctively take responsibility for finding a solution. They refuse to allow their emotions to get in the way of their actions.

Those who shy away from such turbulence are not meant to answer the call. Most followers become frantic not focused. They despair when the call comes and find it much easier to speculate around the water cooler than to articulate what needs to be done, let alone to do it. Reflecting back on my safari excursion, I realize that it's easier to compile data on elephants than to track their habits and locate them in their natural habitat.

Leaders don't sidestep the challenge but get in lockstep with it. They are motivated by finding a way through the challenge, by creating a win-win for all stakeholders, and by using their influence for increased efficiency. The challenges you're facing right now can usher you into a new level of instinctive leadership. The way you respond to the trials of life will reveal what you're made of.

You instinctively know you can lead in the jungles in which you find yourself. Don't allow the criticisms of others or the distractions of the urgent to deter you from your destiny. Instinctive leaders know that they must keep their identity, purpose, and passion before them in order to navigate successfully through the mazes and minefields.

Several years ago when I was taking media training, an instructor told me there's no such thing as a bad question. The only thing that matters in media is the response, not the question. I quickly learned that most journalists ask questions, but they only print answers. The question isn't as newsworthy as the answer. In the same way that a journalist's question pales in significance to the response the interviewee gives, the same is true for this call of opportunity. Life is placing a demand on you. *The demand isn't as significant as your purpose.*

The demands of life don't matter nearly as much as your response; this distinction forms delineation between impressive and inspirational. How will you respond to the challenge in your life right now? Will you merely acquiesce to the issue, succumb to the avoidance of opportunity? Or will you chart your course, stabilize your process, and organize your assets as you take on the challenge before you? When opportunity calls, instinctive leaders answer every time.

From Obstacles to Opportunities

For years I've believed that God usually promotes us to our level of tolerance for pain. So when you whine about being overwhelmed and unable to inspire others to join you, in essence you're saying, "Don't take me any higher. I can't handle any more." Start pushing something that you can't carry and watch how people will come to your aid. But pick up a box you can manage, and people will simply watch you carry the load. Instinctive leadership never retreats from chaotic questions, unreasonable demands, and burdensome boxes.

Most of us carry loads so fragile that there is little room for mishap. However, I evaluate instinctive leaders by their response to troublesome dilemmas. The better you are at responding to a challenge, the more apt you are to succeed. Followers avoid responsibility by avoiding leadership. They have no ramifications as long as they do what they are told. Consequently, their leaders must do the telling. Similarly, a follower obeys directives responsively but rarely takes the initiative to be proactive or to embrace a challenge head on.

Instinctive leaders set the trend. They respond to crises and handle the mishaps of life, minimizing damages and maximizing opportunities. An instinctive leader radiates an air of confidence and composure that attracts and energizes those around them.

People don't follow popularity; they admire it but they don't build on it. They do build, however, on good leadership. Employees often put the house up for sale, pull the kids out of school, and take out a new mortgage in a new city, all because they received a call from an instinctive leader. Since good followers count on sharing a larger vision, a leader without a strategy is like going joyriding in a car without steering. People don't feel safe following someone who doesn't think ahead, creating an enticing vision of success and yet planning for problems.

Instinctive leaders manage the dismal, the distracted, and the dangerous. They view these impositions and oppositions as opportunities to test their strength, exercise their talent, and expand their vision. It is stressful but rewarding, tiring yet tempting. Instinctive leadership finds accomplishment in its ability to navigate a response to challenges by proactive and reactive reasoning.

Life *will* bring challenges. Try all you want to avoid trouble, but you're liable to run into a tornado when running away from a windstorm! Sometimes you can know all that research can teach you and will have memorized all kinds of contingency plans. And yet when trouble strikes, you discover fears you didn't know you had. Instinctive leadership is courage in action. It cuts through the intensity of the crisis and responds with strength, agility, and urgency.

I once employed a security agent who knew volumes of information about law enforcement, protection, and crime prevention. He could teach the role, and he definitely looked the part. However, his intellect could not compensate for weak instincts. When we encountered gunplay at the Dallas–Fort Worth airport, he actually ran off and left me in the middle of the danger!

My security agent was not a bad person, but he simply could not be effective in a reactive situation. He could talk about hypothetical scenarios and classroom defense techniques, but in the heat of real danger, his training went out the window. Needless to say, I replaced him with someone whose knowledge was matched by their instinctive leadership.

Under pressure we have a tendency to go to our default settings. I guess his default instinct was stuck on flight instead of fight. Maybe you or I would've been tempted to do the same in a similar situation; it's fascinating to see what pressure produces in any of us. Sometimes we can't know our instincts from our insecurities until we go from the frying pan into the fire a few times.

While most of us are not placed in life-threatening situations, we do face turmoil that threatens our family, our company, or our income. Whatever the threat, we all face fears every day. When effective leaders are stressed or fearful, they have to rely on their instincts to survive. When the wind blows, whether gentle breeze or bitter blast, you must stand strong.

Leadership Instincts and Attitudes

Our instincts inform the way we've learned to lead. Obviously, our personalities, professional abilities, and social skills contribute to this leadership style that's been developing within us. Most business gurus and leadership experts usually categorize leaders by the way they handle conflict, by the extent they involve others in the decision-making process, and by the priorities that guide their actions. If you want to harness your instincts to lead as effectively as possible, then you need to identify your own natural or default approach to leadership.

From what I've learned about myself, I tend toward what I call a consultative style of leadership. This leader instinctively listens to feedback from his team, studies past and current data, and reflects on research and trends. He or she will ultimately make a decision but not without consulting all available influences to ascertain a course of action that is collaborative. This instinctive leader will ultimately make his own decision but shies away from unresearched conclusions.

Other leadership styles and the instincts that form their basis can be just as effective, depending on the unique strengths of the individual leader. Each different style may also have various blind spots that can sometimes threaten a leader's ability to remain self-aware and vulnerable. Let's consider a few and see if you can identify the one that describes your present instinctive style.

Autocratic style tends toward the propensity of making decisions independent of input. These leaders instinctively already know what they want to do. They are decisive and accept full responsibility for their decisions. These autocratic leaders may factor in other variables but ultimately trust their own hunches and instinctive decisions in leading the organization. They are not easily deterred by the opinions of others and provide a predictable kind of security by their sovereignty.

Leaders with a **chaotic style** bring the team together and empower them to resolve the conflict while distancing themselves from the issue at hand. These leaders instinctively bring the right people together but don't always know how to focus their abilities. A chaotic-style leader develops and empowers those he leads to either form a committee or struggle through the issue to the best of their ability, and then he implements what they decide after the debate has subsided.

The **democratic-style** leader instinctively presides based on the majority's opinions. This leadership style puts issues to a vote and feels comforted by the decision being based on the will of the team. This style often gains buy-in from the team as members feel their voices are reflected in the decision. This leader may persuade his staff to view the issues from a variety of angles, eager to have them think through every possible solution and contingency. Above it all, he desires team unity and wants everyone connected to the decision-making process on a daily basis.

Laissez-faire-style managers serve as mentors and have great motivational skills. They instinctively inspire the team toward excellence but often detach themselves from the actual decision-making processes. They try to hire the best people and then trust them with doing what they were hired to do as well as advancing the organization and its mission. These leaders focus on areas of innovation and future advancement, since they have set up their team to handle the present problems.

Leaders in the **persuasive style** make the decision but will spend a great deal of time convincing and persuading the team that what they have already decided is the best route to take. This leader is a great motivator and uses his or her charm and charisma to assist in creating cohesive teamwork. He instinctively needs the approval of his team and wants them to stand by his decisions and understand why he made them, even if they don't agree.

Though I am instinctively the consultative style leader, I understand the value of choosing a team that has a contribution worth considering. I also understand the value of various styles of leadership, and I have learned that a strong sense of everyone's strengths and weaknesses helps me to determine best-case scenarios, similar to the way a carpenter chooses a tool for the present kind of job he's tackling.

Strong, effective leaders will possess aspects of all these styles and have the discernment to know which will eradicate the problem as well as maximize advancement. They will be well attuned to their instincts so that they can choose the right tool for the job at hand. They know you can't simply be one-dimensional. You must adapt to the prerequisites of any given situation, and having a wide array of options at your disposal increases your confidence, wisdom, and ability to remain calm.

Leadership has never been a one-size-fits-all endeavor, and those who only have one propensity will not be able to handle all issues or work well with all types of people. Being an effective leader requires that you understand what works best in which situation. There is also something to be said by striving to learn what works best with what type of person you are leading.

One of my favorite pieces of wisdom from Scripture comes from Peter's advice about how husbands should relate to their wives. He says, "Dwell with them according to knowledge." Good advice, not just for marriage but for any endeavor in which you seek to nurture relationships and grow together. It's hard to lead someone that you don't understand.

Instincts Aren't on Résumés

A list of accomplishments on paper can never replace an instinctive leader's response to someone sitting across from them. We all know looks can be deceiving. Résumés can be as airbrushed as a model on a magazine cover. In interviews, I don't focus on the page of "facts" in front of me as much as my instinctive response to our conversation. So I question individuals on how they would handle certain situations.

It's important for me to get a sense of not just what they know or which school they attended, but how their mind works and the repository of experience from which they can frame new situations. If you think of a debate in a presidential election, many of the questions are designed to determine not just a candidate's stance but how he or she would handle complicated circumstances.

It's important that you have been formally trained, but that alone doesn't guarantee that when the heat is on you can make judgments and decisions that are well thought out. Anyone who has had their feet on the ground in management knows that textbook answers may pass quizzes, but they don't build companies or churches. Answers on paper do not start companies or manage staffs. Textbook answers don't build results, but good instincts do!

Perhaps my view is skewed by my background, but I prefer leaders who have been in the trenches. I tend to prefer people who know what it means to rise through the ranks and see the organization from a variety of angles and positions. Because I am admittedly a pull-yourself-up-by-the-bootstraps person who worked his way up, always crawling before walking, I value people who have enjoyed wide and diverse experiences, people who have failed and learned something from what went wrong, people who shrugged it off and kept going. Individuals who have followed and taken orders are more balanced at understanding what is a reasonable expectation for those they later lead. Unless you have been there and done that, you have a tendency to have unrealistic expectations. Without a few battle scars and bullet wounds from the trenches, most people have not fully developed their instinctive ability to lead.

Instinctive leadership cannot be reduced to a simple formula or a series of steps. It boils down to an awareness of your instincts, a willingness to trust what they tell you most of the time, and courageously stepping forward to take responsibility. If you want to develop into a more instinctive leader, I encourage you to look for opportunities around you. Ignore the ones outside your areas of passionate interest and invest in the ones already alive within you.

Look for individuals who model this kind of instinctive leadership in your field and ask them to mentor you. Watch what they do as much as you listen to their counsel. Continue growing in self-awareness and understanding of what makes you get out of bed in the morning. Step up, step out, and lead on!

CHAPTER 15

⊰◇⊱

Instincts Don't Stink!

Our guide seemed excited, but I felt nauseous. Pointing to a spot a few feet from our Jeep, he said, "You see that? It means the elephants aren't far!"

"Wow," I said. "More than one?"

"Yes," he said. "Several of them, and at least one is female."

Smelling it before I saw it, I tried to read the information he had ascertained from his rather rank natural source, but, well, let's just say I was a novice.

On my safari I saw many surprising scenes but none more stunning than this one. Off to the left side of our Jeep, amid the brush and branches, loomed a huge pile of, eh, well...a huge pile of animal waste. And when I say "huge," I mean the size of a diesel engine in a semi! Whew—talk about packing some power!

Now, I know you may be shocked that I'm writing

to you about animal dung, but you can't be any more amazed than I was when the zoologist stopped and told me all that we can learn from the droppings animals left behind. In fact, he said that their waste provides a high-tech system of clues revealing the who, what, when, and where of the animals in the region. I never knew something that smells so bad could be so smart!

But the thought of tracking the future by looking at the remains of the past captivated me. If we want an instinctive understanding about where we're going, then we must become aware of what we've left behind. Clues aren't always in the pretty things we've done. Sometimes the greatest insight emerges from the mistakes made and opportunities wasted.

Most psychologists assert that the best predictor of future behavior is past behavior. But this doesn't always mean that you will do the same thing again. However, it does mean that if we want to change and avoid repeating past failures, then we must learn to read our past the same way my guide read what the elephants left behind. I doubt the animals had any idea that they left so many clues about their identity and future behavior. And as crazy as it may sound, I'm convinced that we leave behind the same kinds of clues even if we're unaware of the trail.

Just as a forensic psychologist—or profiler, as they're often called—gets inside the mind of a criminal looking for clues by searching motivations and developing a profile, we must examine the evidence behind us. Call it what you like, but finding out what works and doesn't work in life has a lot to do with understanding ourselves. It isn't enough to examine the hearts and minds of others; we must examine our own, as well.

Mistakes into Motivations

People who have not developed their instincts waste potential and lack tenacity. I see people wasting potential every day because they lack the determined drive to develop their opportunities. To him whom much is given (favor), much is required (tenacity). When the gift is given, you must reinforce your instincts with determination and perseverance.

Often our drives and tenacity come from the places that stink in our lives. The sweet smell of success is often preceded by the sour stench of past mistakes! For me, part of that drive comes from the smelly place of losing my job and having a wife and children to support. Now, that set of circumstances isn't foreign to a lot of people. But for me the stench of losing almost everything left me with a tenacious drive to get up and go forward. Any lackadaisical proclivities that I might have indulged were eradicated by the stench of unemployment, repossessed cars, and unpaid rent. Have you ever gotten a whiff of bankruptcy? Now, that smells bad!

You can see hints of the drive and tenacity even in the disparities of life. Many times it isn't what we're running to that drives us as much as it's what we're running from. What have you left behind that gives you angst and energy, disdain and drive? Perhaps looking at the forensics of your past can catapult you forward in a way that merely dreaming can never attain!

The programs that we offer in my ministry with inmates have had amazing success at helping the misguided redirect their misplaced aggression into motivation. In short, your instincts might be short-circuiting in bad relationships and delinquent behaviors, but by tapping those instincts, you can change what's eating at you into something more productive.

Most of us will find roots for our instincts in our childhood if we're willing to shake the tree. Sometimes our current problems and apparent mistakes occur as a result of ignoring these early cues from childhood. We feel thwarted and blocked by unseen barriers when we try to please others while ignoring our instincts.

And, unfortunately, we often have our instincts conditioned out of us by our practical influencers: parents, siblings, teachers, coaches, pastors, and peers. We're told to "be practical" and to "get real" instead of living by the instinctive truth longing to emerge in our lives.

Others who have used their instincts to succeed are

human like you, flawed like you, and gifted like you. They may have been conditioned by their culture to be someone they were not, someone they had to dismantle in order to access their instinctive identity and natural gifts. So if they used what they had been given, you, too, can use what *you've* been given.

Here are some things to examine *that might give you a clue as to how you got where you are right now.*

Many people seem to have trouble identifying their highest passion and gifting. I often tell them, "Your purpose is in your passions—not just what you love but what you passionately hate." Obviously, some people's passion is exemplified in what they love to do. Their personal preferences and professional proclivities make their positive passions easy to detect. But some people don't realize that sometimes what you cannot stand is also a clue.

If you can't stand to see bad hairdos, maybe you should consider becoming a stylist. If you loathe seeing dilapidated houses and peeling paint, then maybe you should consider being a contractor or interior designer. Does the plight of the homeless make you shudder? Your passion might lead you to work with a nonprofit to eradicate this pervasive problem.

Just as your instinct is your insight, your passion is your instinctive power. Knowing what you love, as well as what you love to hate, can fuel your instincts in ways that provide a superoctane boost to the engine of your success.

Instinctive Time Management

Most people think that being busy equates to being productive. However, many studies suggest that busyness is a sign of poor time management and lack of focus. You become exhausted simply because you're divided! There's no room left for your instincts to operate. You can't hear what your instincts are telling you above the noise clamoring all around you.

Some of the busiest marriages are often the most miserable ones. Some of the hardest-working people in the world are still way underwater and in debt. They may not need more money as much as they need more focus in buying and more focus in what they are building.

So the notion that being busy means you are productive is absolutely not true. In fact, some studies suggest that only 20 percent of what we do every day is our highest and best use. This means that 80 percent of what we do each day could be done by numerous others. And yet the unique contributions that we alone can make only take up 20 percent of our time! Imagine how much more of everything you could have if you switched those stats and spent 80 percent of your time doing what you were created to do and only 20 percent of your time tackling the mundane and ordinary. We spend far too much time investing in areas that are not central to our core purpose and passion.

Some of the most effective people in their field spend a considerable time on the golf course. They aren't always running around with two cell phones and an iPad hanging out of their pocket. They simply focus on what they do best. When they work, they work hard. And when they play, they play just as hard. Curiously enough, they're often more productive, instinctively getting things done even in the midst of leisure activities.

I confess there have been times I was so busy with people and issues I didn't need to handle that when I was genuinely needed for what I alone can contribute, I had exhausted my availability and strength. In those times I didn't segment my best use from my possible use. We must leave our overextended busyness to the dung heap of past mistakes, and concentrate on the sweet, instinctive smell of success!

Making Room for Instincts to Operate

One of the things the zoologist taught me emerges out of the fact that many times when the animals appear to be roaming in the wild, they are still contained by fences. Though the landscape appears to go on for infinity, it has limitations. Though the wild habitat appears natural, the animals are still fenced in. As a result, the gamekeepers and wildlife specialists must burn off excess brush in order to maintain the ecological equilibrium. This brush-burning technique is done to simulate the amount that roaming herds would consume if they weren't fenced in.

If this were not done, the property would become overgrown, resulting in the excess of some plants and animals and the extinction of others. Farmers often use a similar technique to conduct a "controlled burn" on some of their fields. Burning off old crops often adds nitrogen-rich nutrients to the soil and makes it even more fertile for the next planting season.

Obviously, burning off the excess takes skill. The fire has to be intentionally lit and carefully monitored and contained. These burn-offs also help prevent wildfires, since a lightning strike cannot set ablaze an area that has already been scorched and scoured by flames. My guide told me that as odd as it sounds, in this way they use fire to stop fire.

Similarly, we must use directed effort to control misdirected effort. If you're consumed by busyness at the expense of real business, perhaps you should set a new and different kind of fire. When you burn off the clutter of busyness and leave yourself time to think and study, you may get less done, but the things you do will be far more productive and ultimately more organic to what you are passionate about accomplishing.

The fringe benefit of burning off the brush is a much clearer view of the terrain ahead. No one can see beyond their sight lines. And when cluttered with obstructions, our vision will always be impaired. So before we move forward, I call on your instinctive imagination to answer a few questions.

Where do you need to clear a path so that you have room to maneuver toward your ultimate destination?

What needs to be burned away in order to refine what you're focused on finding?

How can you unblock your view of who you are, what you could be, and where you could go?

My friend, take control of your life and subdue the earth you have been given, then burn off the clutter and chart the next years of your life. Once you can see the ground beneath your feet again, follow the bread crumbs that your instincts have been scattering! It's time to launch yourself into your destiny. From here on, your path is clear and the sky is blue. And remember, watch where you're going and keep your nose to the wind—you never know when you might encounter what an elephant left behind!

CHAPTER 16

Balancing Intellect and Instinct

Many people live lives that are in poor rotation, which consequently impedes their mobility, because they don't balance what they know with what they sense. You see, in order to travel at our maximum velocity, we must balance the power of our intellect with the truth of our instincts.

Information, here referred to as intelligence, in its purest form is irreplaceable in leadership as well as in life. I don't merely mean one's IQ as much as I mean the necessary access to relevant data, pertinent information, and the understanding to interpret it correctly. As essential as instincts are to exploring the design of your destiny, you must not ignore the facts for the feelings!

Balancing what you know in your mind with what

you know in your heart takes practice. This kind of instinctive intelligence requires walking a tightrope between what is verifiable and what is intangible. Successful people use instinct with intellect to make each one more useful. Without access to intelligence, one cannot develop policy or maintain order. And yet nothing you've read should replace your reliance upon instinct to inform the decisions you make.

The two must work in sync. If your gut feeling contradicts the facts, then ask people you trust to weigh in before you ignore the objective information at hand. Use what you know and what you sense to arrive at a more synthesized decision, one that integrates both objective and subjective realities.

While instincts may be the compass that gives direction, intelligence guides the process through which that transition can be realized. No one can make great decisions if they have poor information. The greater your efforts at understanding data, the more likely you are to liberate your instincts. Whether you're forging alliances with corporations or governments, churches or clubs, investors or stockholders, you can't quantify value purely based on instinct. Data has significant placement in determining value and timing of transactions and interactions.

On the other hand, always relying on the probability of progress by what appears on paper will not ensure success. Our instincts are informed by the data we feed it. Sometimes we don't realize how much more we actually know about risk assessment until we look beyond the facts.

Part of the impetus for writing this book was derived from sitting between the zoologist, whose intellect inspired me, and the Zulu guide, whose instincts forever changed me, on a safari. Seeing the significance and uniqueness of both roles in the wild opened my eyes to the universal truth in this metaphor. Not only does a wise person balance instincts with intellect, they must also make sure that the intelligence they're using comes from reliable sources with balanced perspectives.

Balancing Acts

Finding the balance between intellect and instinct can take many forms, depending on your own unique considerations and contexts. For instance, I've had the privilege of working with a couple of ladies who are both public relations experts and yet couldn't be more different. As they have each done work for me over the years, each has become personal friends of our family as well.

Knowing them personally as well as professionally has only emphasized how different they are. One of them is from a very conservative political background. Before meeting me, she had never been exposed to an

African-American whose background was so different from her own. The other lady, also African-American, is morally conservative but politically liberal. I don't think they could agree on which side of the street to walk down on many issues.

Though they are both dear friends, having them both comment on an issue is like watching Fox News and MSNBC at the same time! Hearing them both always produces fireworks, and I love it! Their combined counsel has been a tremendous resource, providing a unique barometer from their constituency for each decision I contemplate. I cannot tell you how beneficial it has been to hear their varied perspectives on my pending decisions. Sitting between their ideas and input has helped me find the right balance and allowed me to balance the intelligence they provide with my instinctive response to it.

If you are sincerely interested in a balanced truth, you can't be fed biased data. You need multiple points of view in order to see the big picture. Being able to determine principles from propaganda has been very important for me as a leader. There is always somebody who's trying to use my mouth to convey his or her message. The only way to avoid becoming someone else's mouthpiece is by channeling information from a variety of sources. If all the people with whom you associate sound like you, vote like you, dress like you, and think like you, then you have no litmus test to evaluate your instincts.

Blind Spots

Perhaps you've heard the story about a group of blind men who unknowingly encountered an elephant. Each of the four moved cautiously toward the creature to discern him by touch. One of them touched his massive ears and said, "This beast is flat and flexible—like a palm leaf!"

The second grabbed the massive leg of the elephant and, amazed at its circumference and texture, proclaimed, "No, he is sturdy and round like a tree trunk!"

The third blind man grabbed hold of the elephant's tail and said, "You are both wrong! This creature is thin and wiry as a snake."

The last blind man, leaning against the side of the mighty beast, said, "You are all as stupid as you are blind! This animal is strong and sturdy, like a stone wall."

Obviously, each of the blind men walked away thinking he knew what the elephant looked like by touching it. But in reality he had only encountered one part, a small unique piece of its whole body. Talk about not knowing your blind spots! It's no wonder then that this story, which originated in ancient India, has been recounted in so many different cultures and religions.

The timeless truth of the blind men and the elephant remains keenly relevant in our understanding of balance. So much of what informs our opinions is based on where we touch the subject. Do we see the whole elephant or just the small part we can touch?

When someone advises you, always know what part of the elephant this person is touching. Don't build plans around a description that is, in fact, a narrow perspective based on touching one side of a much more global and massive reality. I've always known that each of the two ladies I mentioned informs me from a different side of the elephant. But when I interact with both, I can balance their perspectives and descriptions and judge what I should do without taking either's description to be representative of the whole. As it was with my zoologist and my Zulu friend, sitting between instincts and information helped me to have balance.

For me, this is a very inspirational place to be. While in between them, I'm able to navigate more effectively and be much more flexible. When you consider how intellect and instinct work together, you progress that much further toward accomplishing the goals of the champion you were meant to be. If a person ignores comprehensive data, then he is going forward in partial blindness. Imagine having the instincts to buy a piece of property but not having an appraisal done over that land. That's foolish, right? Absolutely.

As instincts might reveal to you that this is the right land to buy, information tells you what to bid based on trends in the marketplace. Information tells you about the schools in the area and the comparable properties that were sold in its neighborhood. Information shows you the age of the property and who owned it before you. These variables are all significant to success.

Intelligence must influence decision making. Too many times I've seen people who move forward on whims and later regret the decision they made. As important as your instinct is as a tool, don't exclude the other tools at your disposal. Generally, the instincts initiate the process that information validates.

Occasionally, I've gone with my instinct over information because my feeling to proceed was so strong. The writing of my first book, *Woman, Thou Art Loosed!*, comes to mind. Publishers resisted funding a book in the faith market that addressed women's emotional and spiritual needs from a first-time male author. No comparable data could be found to predict sales. No barometer existed by which they could determine sales or even project print runs.

In spite of this data—or, rather, the lack of it—I went with my instincts and published the book myself. And literally millions of lives have now been touched through that book! There are times you have to go with your gut!

But more often than not, you want your instincts and your intelligence to have a collaborative exchange, with each enhancing the other. The combined influence of these two collaborative agents gives you a well-rounded perspective through which you can lessen the likelihood of mistakes and regret. Don't make one obsolete for the sake of the other, but rather develop a more perfect union, a stronger whole than either singular part can provide on its own.

Instinctive Flexibility

In order to establish balance between intellect and instinct, you need agility and flexibility. Like a tightrope walker tilting one way and then another, compensating here and readjusting there, you must stay loose and responsive. The power of instinct-driven success relies on your ability to adjust and adapt. Instinctive leadership relies on this same dexterity.

Instinctive flexibility requires what I call "360-degree thinking." Being flexible includes the understanding that anything you do affects everyone connected to you. Thinking in a panoramic way of all who will be affected by each move you make allows you to prepare your network in advance. Furthermore, you have no right to expect people to comply with a vision you haven't shared and an expectation you haven't articulated.

For example, I've told several leaders who wanted to pastor that their preparations must extend beyond their own ambitions. It's not just a matter of whether they feel equipped and ready; what about their wife, their children, their finances, their business, their employees, their reputation, and their communities? It isn't just a matter of your being ready for the performance.

If you are contemplating a move or a transition of

any kind, process all variables instinctively before making the final decision. Think through the options, possibilities, and contingencies. No one would plant a garden and not prepare the soil. The tools one uses to harvest must be purchased before one begins to plant. Are we going to can the vegetables or freeze them? Sell them at the farmer's market or give them to neighbors?

In other words, do we have a strategy that anticipates all the variables, or are we only focused on our own accomplishment? Who would have a baby and not prepare the house? It's simply a matter of preparing your life for the new arrival of what's next in your life. Parents usually start stocking shelves, baby-proofing the house, preparing the right room, purchasing baby monitors, assembling cribs, registering for schools and day care, and so much more.

Or why would someone marry a man who was a great date without considering him being a great husband and father? Does he have a job? Does he like children? You can see how the 360-degree concept works. Go full circle and look at your new endeavor from all angles.

In my staff development training, the same approach is important to us. We learned that not considering everything is the equivalent of not considering anything. Some of the best and brightest people I know aren't prepared for the increase that comes from following their instincts. They may have a great backup plan that manages crises but may not have a strategy for success.

If you don't think in a circle, you will leave some area unprotected. Imagine a city with a protective wall in front of a few areas but with vulnerable holes exposed in just as many other areas. Wherever planning ends, problems begin!

Might I suggest that you sit down with a piece of paper and write down the idea? Draw a circle around the idea and write down every person, place, or thing needed to bring your dream to life. You may be shocked by how many individuals need to be in the delivery room for a great idea to be born!

Finally, if you inform, inspire, and impart to all those persons affected, you won't find yourself having to compensate for poor planning by working all the posts you never assigned in advance. When people are prepared—that is, *pre* (in advance) *pared* (cut into the shape of the need)—things move smoothly.

You may not be able to give all those around you the instincts you have. But it is imperative that you share the information. If they have the information and you have the instincts, your goals will not only be achieved—they will exceed anything you have imagined!

CHAPTER 17

Instinctive Relationships

Our instincts remind us that we are social creatures, made to be in relationship to others. You aren't meant to dwell alone. You're made to be in relationship for your own fulfillment and the enhancement of your ever-expanding community.

However, instead of maximizing the strength of our social bonds, we often allow social constructs and expectations to limit us. Whether these are imposed on us by society, our culture, our families, or our own perceptions and misperceptions, we frequently miss the mark of maximum impact and muddle through mediocrity! Too often, we limit ourselves and create barriers, visible and invisible, to opportunities around us.

But this is not how we were made! Like the lions of the field and the eagles of the air, we were born without the inhibition of constructs. Most animals dwell in groups, whether packs, prides, herds, flocks, or convocations. Yet the lions don't try to fly nor the eagles try to run through the wild!

We must stay true to our instincts. Our ultimate instinct is always freedom—freedom of thought, freedom of passion, and freedom of purpose. Too often we try to be what we are not! Soaring without limits is one thing, but we are the only species that has built fences and barriers, restrictions and walls. Man was the inventor of prisons both literal and figurative! You'll never fulfill your destiny until you break out of the constructs and move beyond the socially induced systems that define and limit what is within you!

Cast Your Net

Living successfully by instinct requires a variety of complementary talents and abilities working in harmony to achieve results beyond what you could achieve by sheer talent or hard work alone. As we've discussed, you must build teams and lead them instinctively toward the focused objectives you've established.

But instinctive living will also extend beyond your employees, coworkers, and casual acquaintances. Follow your instincts, and you will encounter people from a wide spectrum of professional and personal endeavors. Typically, we call this networking. And if you think about it, nets are woven from strings going in different directions, tied together at points of connectivity. Human nets must work the same way!

If you network only with people who do what you do and have what you have, then there's no intersection of variations. You might make a nice mop or wig, but you won't have a net that benefits the world! Networks are built on strands that cross lines and make connections in spite of facing different directions or diverse perspectives.

Nets can capture, contain, and convey more than any single string from which they're woven. Fishing with a single line may be fun, but it is always a slow process. More times than not, Jesus used people who handled a net and not a line. There's a benefit in working with a net that a single line can never touch: the potential to increase effectiveness by diverse associations.

Instincts Beyond Borders

If we were to consider your new relationships as diverse territories—similar to what I saw on my safari—then you would soon learn that natural elements do not recognize the boundaries that we often impose. Imagine a rainfall that stays only on your parcel of land. It's not likely. Or an earthquake that stopped at a property line. This isn't normal. Boundaries are sometimes necessary, but they can also limit your ability to fulfill the destiny that your instincts know is possible. These silos must be leveled and these constructs must be crossed if you're going to exceed the usual exploits of people who remain contained by rules rather than become empowered by potential.

Our instincts often lead us across lines to make new connections. It's wise to know where the line is, but if you stay only on your side, then it's a prison! If animals in the jungle stayed on one side of a boundary, then they might as well be in a cage at the zoo. On the other hand, we should not just go thundering into a new territory without any sense of what we're getting into.

Or think of this instinct for boundary crossing this way: whenever there's a question about land boundaries, it's customary to have a survey done to determine where one property ends and the other begins.

These surveys assist in determining who owns which pieces of land and therefore who's responsible for various expenses from taxation to maintenance. No smart person would just buy new territory and only take the seller's words. You would do your homework to understand where the property begins and ends, discover what's on the land, conduct an environmental analysis to study what is under the surface of the soil. Yet I frequently see people who walk into new relationships without giving any research to the nuances of what's next. To not prepare for the new territory is almost disrespectful of the opportunity.

Surveying your property not only reveals boundaries but also includes topography of the land and geographic indicators such as underground water, mineral deposits, and unseen flaws such as seismic fault lines. Most of the time, busy people don't take that same time and deliberation to survey their lives and identify opportunities in their relationships for shared goals, common interests, and mutual benefits. Everything in your life will touch other territories, and I want to help you navigate to broaden your territory!

Instincts Inspire

As an instinctively creative person, sooner or later you will come up with an innovative idea that exceeds the parameters of where you've been before. You start out trying to accomplish something that is within your scope, and soon you are beyond the borders of your territory. During this journey of forging new partnerships and wrangling new relationships, I want to share with you the tools you need to go beyond the known maps of the past. These four basic principles will help you manage the opportunities that exceed the boundaries that you or others have placed on you.

First, you must consider your *inspiration*. If you have something on the inside that instinctively inspires you beyond those around you, this will help you understand why you don't fit. People who are meant to lead have trouble being satisfied with those who seek the normal and are satisfied with the status quo. Their inspirations instinctively take them beyond barriers and lead them to color outside the lines.

Inspiration springs from an instinct, an internal compass, that points across familiar lines toward the unknown. Like a spark kindling tinder into a flame, inspiration ignites you to act on what you envision in your imagination. Others may encounter the same external stimuli but fail to have it inspire them with new ideas or innovative approaches. Those who balance their intellects with instinct know that inspiration is often their offspring.

Your mind takes in data, performs due diligence, and processes information. But your instinct converts knowledge to power. Your instinctive deductive reasoning becomes inspired. It guides your quest to move beyond the scope of those accomplishments of ordinary people and will likely require you to blaze trails and cut through fences.

Inspiration is such a powerful tool and explains some of the way our intelligence complements our instincts. We take in information as raw material, as fuel, and then our instincts shape it into the best form for our current needs. This ability to adapt what we know externally with what we know internally yields the inspiration to bridge the two.

Whether we call it a hunch, an intuition, or a crazy idea, inspiration creates a fire that can provide heat, warmth, and energy to a situation that otherwise remains cold and flat.

Inspiration in Action

Inspiration alone, of course, is not enough. Even if you can express your idea without the help of others, you still face your own limited resources. In other words, you can't catch big fish in shallow water! You have to leave the shore and venture into deeper waters if you want to cast a net that can catch the big fish.

For example, perhaps you started out to produce music, but in the process of producing you soon ran into needing distribution. Most people would either see that as a limitation or simply see the goal as beyond the scope of reasonable possibility. But forming alliances outside of your scope is how you make things happen! I'm amazed at the people who produce books or music that ends up sitting in the attic because the artists can't seem to forge a deal beyond the scope of being a great singer or writer.

Talent is not enough. You can sing like an angel, but you need to think like an elephant if you're going to move beyond where you are. Too many people waste their talent through timidity, afraid to move beyond that which is easy for them to do. For example, I have a friend who is an amazing baker. While excellent at what she does, soon she discovered that with excellence comes opportunity. Her special order catering for private events grew until she was forced to move from her kitchen at home into an industrial kitchen she rented. From there, she carried her cookies to a TV network, and soon the orders were flying in so fast that she needed to go to manufacturers and distribution companies to keep up with demands.

Finally, she hit a wall. She walked away from a great opportunity because she didn't have the cash flow to enlarge her business to the size of its potential demand. She refused to consider getting investors, because the prospect intimidated her.

For me, it was as sad as burying a loved one to see a dream die because the dreamer didn't know how to survey the possibilities and forge relationships beyond her comfort zone. She reached a crossroads where she had to choose between scaling back or including other stakeholders who could take her to the next level and across the fence into new, unknown territory. My friend allowed her fear to dilute her dream.

Whenever you seek to forge relationships that will increase your impact and influence, it begins by surveying the possibilities and then acknowledging your deficiencies. Don't be afraid to acknowledge when something is too big for you. But by the same token, just because you can't do it alone doesn't mean that you can't facilitate it if you can find stakeholders willing to share the risk.

You don't have to buy the land, or invest the capital

for expansion, or become a major distributor in order to benefit from alliances with people who do what you don't do. In fact, I see far too many people who expend all of their energies connecting with people who only duplicate what they do, rather than building alliances with those who can transform their limitations into efficiencies. The art of such alliances is finding the connection between what they do and what you need.

Instincts Intersect

This artful arrangement of alliances forms our second major tool, which I call *intersections*. Finding the intersection points among diverse associations provides the key to maximizing the opportunities God has given you. Like a driver who wants to reach a certain destination, you can't arrive there without making some turns at crucial intersections. On the highway, we find an intersection when an east-to-west road crosses a north-to-south road. Two routes running in different directions briefly meet and cross at this point of mutual contact. Neither road changes directions, but travelers benefit from this connection because it enables them to reach new destinations.

When you follow your instincts, you will find yourself at the intersection of needing to build alliances with people who complete you rather than people who compete with you. Completion occurs when you join forces with others who may not be going your way, but their vision and yours find an intersection and the relationship is built on what connects you rather than alienates or divides you.

Find the touchpoints of what you have in common with people, and don't be so inclined to focus on what divides you. Again, you can't make a turn until you find the corner. This place of connection is what I'm calling the intersection of ideas and inspiration. If we build on what unites us rather than focusing on what divides us—whether in a family, a church, or a business—we can achieve amazing goals with unlikely people because we understand the power of an intersection.

This process is the same no matter the scale or number of participants. Government and church intersect at the place of human needs. Business and philanthropy have different goals until they recognize the benefits from collaborations; big business needs a tax benefit and not-for-profits need funding. Suddenly, their interests intersect. But if they only focused on the major difference between them, then they would both lose out on mutually beneficial opportunities.

You will miss these kinds of benefits if you forge alliances only with those who do what you do. When a social service has a need, the survey says business can supply that need without changing its core. Our church's outreach to former inmates needs our relationships with rental property owners so that we can help one transition to the other. The former inmates need housing; the property owners need consistent tenants. It isn't that they won't take people who have been incarcerated. They don't want to take on the screening process of better determining who's really rehabilitated enough to be trusted to lease. Working with families, social services, and other rehabilitation organizations, we can provide that screen.

Even people within the same fields of study must work together to resolve larger problems than either could tackle alone. While both are scientists, a psychologist's role is different from a psychiatrist's and a neurologist's. One may realize that a patient has a neurological problem that no amount of counseling or medication will resolve. The patient progresses or declines based on their physician's ability to find an intersection with other professionals who don't provide what they do in order to benefit the patient's well-being. Such collaborative efforts work only when you're broad enough in your scope to survey outside of your skill set!

Many unlikely bedfellows find strength when they learn to capitalize on their differences. Business partnerships, social relationships, and marriages all benefit from respecting and integrating each other's differences rather than trying to override them.

My wife is an introvert and I am primarily an extrovert. I've learned not to try and make her refuel in the crowd, and she's learned not to try and make me lie down and refuel in solitude. I hate naps and she hates noise! Yet still we're able to complement each other as we've found the intersections in our uniqueness. Thank God I didn't marry someone like me—our kids would've been left home alone!

If your creativity is free to roam, it will inevitably grow to an intersection where you must recognize the differences and respect them. In order to build these alliances based on the intersection of common goals, you have to be willing to understand the uniqueness of each other's structures and form unions for the greater good.

Yes, you can achieve good things and stay within your yard to do it. But if you're interested in the greater good, you will have to learn how to operate in different arenas. The broader your world becomes, the more flexible you must be in adapting to social constructs that play by different rules.

Instincts Integrate

Now, once we've found the intersection of common needs, we must look for the proverbial win-win, a convergent strategy encompassing the desired outcomes of all stakeholders, which I call *integration*. Whether in business, marriage, or other areas of life, alliances work only when both parties' needs are met and respected in a cross-section of opportunity.

An integration of expectations is the goal we want to pursue.

In this pursuit, the art of negotiation becomes an essential tool. You don't have to be Warren Buffett to need to understand the power of negotiation. Those who negotiate from a selfish perspective of getting what they want at any cost, without integrating a plan that includes and respects others' needs, will always fail. An integrated strategy inherently addresses each individual party's motives, agendas, and goals in the midst of their larger, shared goal. This integration-based strategy includes the fulfillment of those needs in such a way that all differences are respected without losing sight of the ultimate objective.

Also, allow me to explain the crucial difference between merely tolerating these differences versus integrating them. The term *tolerance* is, in my view, deeply overrated. Tolerating differences might be an expression of political correctness, but in order for people to feel fulfilled in life, they must be much more than tolerated. They must feel that their talents, resources, and needs are an integral part of the planning. No one feels comfortable when they're merely tolerated. Toleration tends to be a temporary token. Most people can tolerate for only so long before their patience wears thin and shreds the garment of acceptance they gave to others.

If you want to be successful and outrun and out-think the herd, then you must negotiate by respecting differences and accommodating them in such a way that people feel that their uniqueness isn't just tolerated but is respectfully integrated into the plan. Women in the corporate world appreciate employers who include paid maternity leave and child care. Such benefits will not be used by all, but their inclusion indicates an awareness of personal needs that cannot be ignored. All employees, both female and male, respect employers with an appreciation for cultivating and keeping the best talent in the company.

An integration of participants' needs and desires must be an integral part of any union in order for it to succeed. Including me without integrating what you know to be my needs as a spouse, a partner, a customer, an employee, or just a colleague ultimately dooms our relationship. If you're going to broaden your circle, you must change your thinking to integrate my objectives with your own. Without this component, the other individual, auxiliary, or company will only feel violated by the association, and the opportunity will eventually dissolve.

Instincts Execute

Finally, the fourth and perhaps most vital step is *execution*. A net doesn't work until it's thrown. No fisherman would make a net for fishing and leave it on the boat. You must know how to leverage your alliances by turning your integration strategy into action points. Execution is critical for accomplishment. If you don't execute the plans you have in place, it doesn't matter how inspired you may be, it doesn't matter how meticulously you look for the common touchpoints of integration, and it doesn't even mean much if you integrate my needs into your plans. Inspiration without execution will always lead to frustration.

Whenever I look across the field and see beyond my line of achievement, it always means that relationship will be the bridge that takes me there. If I build the relationship on proposals and promises but fail to execute what I predicted, it won't be long before I've lost my opportunity to play on the wider field. If you can't learn to be a part of the team and transform ideas into actions, then ideas become worthless.

I can't tell you how many times I've been in a meeting or with a group of bright, creative, talented people who get stuck in their own ideas. Their ideas may seem good and some great, but without execution it's ultimately impossible to evaluate the worth of an idea. In order for your innate ability to produce a product, create a craft, or establish an industry, you must have action points.

What needs to happen in order for this marketing campaign to have the major impact we want it to have for our product? Who's going to design the pop-up ads? Who's going to determine which sites they go on? Who's going to buy radio airtime? Who's going to make sure all the ads align with the same theme and consistent language? Who's going to follow up with consumer awareness groups? And on and on the process goes, until all pieces are in place.

Your ability to transform inspiration into an intersection where integration takes place will only be as powerful as your execution. And eventually, your ability to execute will become a matter of integrity. Are you known for having good ideas but not being able to follow through? For overpromising and underdelivering? Or will you be known as someone who not only follows your instincts for excellence but exchanges them for action and carries out decisions once you've made them? Especially with collaborative efforts, which we've seen are usually the most effective, it's an incredible breach of trust to other stakeholders when any individual does not do his or her part in the process. Everyone does their part in order to achieve the large-scale results that will benefit them all.

An instinct without execution is only a regret. As we've seen, all of us have the ability to achieve more by harnessing our intellect to our instincts. We need other people—more than just the usual suspects. Extend your net and make it work in new and instinctive ways—you might be surprised what you can catch!

CHAPTER 18

✜

Juggling by Instinct

The most frequent question I am asked when interviewed is "How do you manage so many different things at the same time?" When I try to explain, the best metaphor I can devise is that of the juggler. The art of juggling requires tossing two or more objects in a rhythmic sequence so that they continue moving without hitting the ground.

If you hold one object in your hand and toss it in the air, it's not really juggling. You're just tossing a ball. A juggler manages to keep objects airborne in a smooth, even flow that utilizes gravity in sync with his own dexterity. He keeps giving each object just enough of a push so that all items remain suspended and none falls out of sequence. If you hope to live by your instincts, then you must recognize that you will be a juggler.

How does this happen? Have you ever heard the

phrase "one thing leads to another"? This also holds true about the many worlds that you have to manage as you progress and take on new initiatives. Whether you are broadening your horizons or your current responsibilities are broadening you, life demands more to play every day! If you conquer one space, it creates opportunity and responsibility in other spaces and places. If you follow your instincts, it not only opens up the arena you're pursuing, but it also expands your possibilities into other arenas you didn't originally anticipate.

Many people don't realize that instincts are not just a key to the next dimension; they're more like the master key that opens up new worlds beyond your wildest dreams. What feels enclosed by huge trees and massive shrubbery keeps going and opens up into an expanse leading to plains, rivers, and mountains. Every meadow is adjacent to another, so as you step into the one you expected, it will also be interconnected with others that you might not have anticipated.

Everything you touch is touching something connected to it. This connectivity is crucial to understand no matter what the field. Points of contact are used to measure the impact of marketing. Relational networks transmit the energy for global economics. Connections serve as catalysts for collaborations and corporations. Our technological connectivity has produced social networks that continue to cause some companies to rise and some to collapse. Opportunities, like the information highway itself, move at warp speed! If you understand the touch points, you can be far more effective than ever before.

Common Denominators

In my case, I have movie sets that require me for film production. I have my writing, which is both an avocation as well as a vocation. I have my speaking that I do from time to time on college campuses for leadership conferences. I have my ministry through the church and the pastoral team I enjoy leading. I have preaching, which is my calling and my heart. There's the music label I own and the occasional plays I produce. Those responsibilities would split me apart if I didn't find what holds them together. In my case, the common denominator is communication.

Lay out your life and the jungles you operate in like a map on an excursion, and plan the trip. I'll bet if you find the common denominators, you can manage to get your hands on everything, touching it at least long enough so it has your brand on it. One thing they all share is you! What else do you see that unites them? If you are involved in them and effective at them, there is something common to them that connects the jungles!

Global thinkers and instinctive leaders keep the forty-thousand-foot view in sight while managing to keep their feet on the ground—at least sometimes.

They are persons whose lives or talents have taken them to a level at which new doors open into new areas of influence, and all of them require some time investment to manage.

Of course, you don't have to juggle if you outsource control to other companies or persons and rely on their efficiency to manage areas that are not central to your core objectives. This can make your life less complicated, but it will also make your life less profitable and give you less ability to determine the outcome. It's like hiring someone to raise your children; it may make your life less complicated, but it gives you less influence over the outcome.

Growth requires that you manage many things, appear many places, and evolve constantly in a reactionary way to the demands that are birthed through the opportunities you have been given. Now, in truth we are all limited resources, so the first thing one must do is decide what opportunity will get your time and how much time is required to make that work efficiently.

You don't have to build a farm, start a company, or run a university to get the rhythm of management and juggle responsibilities. Anyone who cooks knows that cooking has a rhythm. This sauce cooks for this long, so while it's simmering stir the other. Yes, good cooks have rhythm and they know how to juggle. The roast is in the oven while the potatoes are soaking. The table is set while the soup simmers. Pacing is everything in cooking!

In business sessions I have always taught that if you make a living doing something that requires your hands, your business is automatically limited by your having only two hands. You simply cannot micromanage everything and expect to thrive. But the adept juggler keeps all items moving by giving each of them enough attention to keep them in rotation.

Whole Wide World

If you have the kind of personality, product, or mission that excels, you will inevitably find yourself operating in several different jungles at the same time. The Bible says, "A man's gift will make room for him, and brings him before great men" (Prov. 18:16). If you follow your instincts and apply your intellect, your success will lead to new doorways of destiny and new windows of worldwide wonder.

From my experience and observation, this expansion of ideas and opportunities often occurs more frequently when you're focused on excellence in only one arena at first. People who take a shotgun approach and rush at everything available cannot maintain focus and gain enough momentum to succeed in any area. Ironically, when you deliberately try to take on multiple jungles, you may not learn to survive in any of them!

Growth isn't always a result of exceeding boundaries, as much as it is shared interests and the common square of shared space. Consider the way business needs are interconnected and therefore conglomerates emerge. World markets ebb and flow and create economic tides that pour from one culture to another. Even in our shopping malls, retailers share common facilities to attract shared consumers.

The economics of the world are so interconnected that economic shifts in one country affect countries around the world. Now brokers have to be bilingual—if not speaking multiple languages—in order to be competitive as their conversation is no longer communal but global. The brokers must be concerned about what's happening beyond their borders primarily because the borders touch. They don't just touch geographically but interculturally and relationally. So as they learn the language of the worlds they touch, they increase advancement and improve efficiency. The message is clear: you can no longer stay in your lane and compete in the race!

Highly instinctive people have more to learn than the nuances of their home base. They must be astute at knowing more about the worlds they touch and how to understand the languages, cultural systems, and best business practices to meet those needs with proficiency and understanding. I can guarantee you, every action you make is touching more than who you think. You must realize that what you do in your corner affects the whole house, as we are all inextricably interconnected.

From One Jungle to the Next

Discovering the interconnectivity of your various jungles as you launch into new adventures of self-discovery will only enhance your journey. On a personal level, once you leave your cage, you are less likely to allow limits to define possibilities ever again. Beyond personal experience, you discover an overarching sense of purpose and destiny that guides you beyond your territory. Listening to your instincts gives you one of the best chances to make a real and meaningful difference in the world around you.

The ground you walk upon reverberates with the decisions you make and echoes with your lifestyle choices. Like anything that spreads by touch, instinctive influence cannot be contrived, controlled, or regulated. Your instincts will take you over the border and across the fence, and with them come collaboration and cooperation. Once you have a sense of living by instinct, you will amass unlikely teams, connecting people, places, and things in a way others before you have never imagined.

Before long, your simultaneous environments will

align like spokes in a wheel that has you as its hub. And as your circle of contacts continues to enlarge, you will be able to cover more ground with each revolution.

But this is not about turning the wheel faster or winning a race; it's about your direction, your purpose. Connectivity must not be used to inflame the greedy or empower the selfish. It provides a guide to unearthing your power to function in a pluralistic society in various orbits for a purpose greater than yourself. It is this pursuit of your purpose and passions that lands you in a broader context, exploring new possibilities and challenging limitations. It is an awareness of the way fulfilling your own destiny allows others to fulfill theirs, both through example and through connection.

Roaming Notification

When I was preparing to travel to South Africa, I was reminded of the need to contact my cell phone service provider and notify them to activate international coverage. While some carriers have comprehensive plans, many of them vary the rates depending on the specific countries where I would be traveling. Like a cell phone, your gifts will work in other jungles, other countries, and other arenas. So understand the challenge is not about your gifts, personality, or talent operating in other settings as much as it about how to access those multiple settings simultaneously.

Where are your instincts leading you? Your first step in learning to juggle settings smoothly may be looking ahead and anticipating where you might be heading. Although you never know where your instinctive gifts may lead, this doesn't mean that you don't set your GPS on a destination! Look around the corner and consider where you want to be in six months, two years, a decade from now.

You can never begin this process too early. Even as children, the dreams we had and the direction provided by our parents and mentors often set us on a trajectory for triumph. I am forever grateful for the amazing foresight my parents had in allowing me to visit places and stations in life beyond where I began. Though our family had modest means, we didn't have impoverished dreams. So my parents planted seeds for success in myself and my siblings whenever they could.

They drove us through beautifully manicured neighborhoods and pointed out exquisite homes where they knew they would never live. They allowed us to taste gourmet cuisine, listen to operas, watch ballets, and reflect on artistic masterpieces. Now, we couldn't stay long or eat much, but my parents knew that you can't evolve into what you won't explore. They knew we couldn't stay there at that time, but they wanted us to glimpse how our future could unfold. They wanted our instinctive talents to roam beyond our present coverage!

You see, freedom is often as much a state of mind as it is a state of being. They liberated us to know what was out there in hopes it might ignite something inside us that we could be or do. They didn't know where we would end up or the ways in which our worlds would expand and evolve. They probably didn't consider that everything we touch leads us to a new gateway for future success. They simply knew that they wanted to enlarge our world.

And Is More

As we learn to juggle, we often misperceive the bandwidth of our abilities. We mistakenly think we must eliminate or compromise one jungle in order to enter another. But here's the news flash: this isn't either-or!

Many times people choose what's next at the expense of forsaking what is. You could start a business *and* keep your career. You could explore your passion for music *and* start a family. You could remain on the corporate ladder *and* pursue completing your college degree. Not either-or but *and*!

It is possible to add without subtracting. If you add infrastructure to increase, you end up with empires that empower more than you can imagine! The idea of managing more intimidates some people, because they add by subtracting. Their way is to add this, take away that, and basically trade one for the other. They forget about creative, strategic moves that adapt to *and*.

Your cup is supposed to run over. It not only overflows with abundance in your own life, but into the lives of those around you. Your ability to juggle multiple worlds directly affects your community— producing new jobs, new ideas, and new universities.

Universities? Yes! Not necessarily the institutions of higher learning that typically come to mind, but a collection of people learning from one another. A university is simply a community of teachers and students, experts and apprentices working together, or, as it's expressed in Latin, *universitas magistrorum et scholarium*. The prevailing notion is that the up-and-comers learn from those ahead of them.

Learning from the masters prevents becoming enslaved! Most highly successful and accomplished people have mastered many worlds, which I'm calling "jungles" here. When we look to these people as role models, mentors, and teachers, we receive juggling lessons!

If you use this principle even on a small scale, it will bring order to your chaos and change the way you perceive obstacles on your path. More opportunity emerges when you organize a cluttered life. You can be philanthropic *and* profitable, work *and* volunteer, raise children *and* have a career, if you catch the principle. You can add to what you have without losing what you've accomplished, if you stop holding everything so tightly and simply learn to juggle!

Diversify Your Dreams

Your life should be as diverse as your interests. Think of the diversity exhibited in a shopping mall: one building with diverse stores but shared cost and leadership. A mall is the gathering of many stores around one common location. Look at what combined strengths do to marketing, management, security needs, customer traffic, and parking—a mall houses the seemingly unrelated under one roof and manages them all in spite of their diversity.

The one-roof concept unifies diversity. Finding the one roof, or in other words the points of connectivity, is essential to bring better management and faster movement to your life. To understand what's touching the things you touch will help you move laterally and not take crazy leaps into wild choices. One of those points of connectivity in your world is you. You are the shared interest. You are the ultimate brand. But there may be others, so keep looking.

In the case of the mall, we see many. They all need lights and heat, air-conditioning and maintenance. They all need management and, most important, they all need people. When you find what's common in your life, it lowers stress and organizes the future.

And you don't have to be the Galleria or the Mall of America to benefit from organizing the diverse interests into a structurally sound whole. Successful stores don't discard what brought them success even as they innovate for what's before them.

The demands on your life don't have to be identical to be interrelated. That passion you have, the vibrancy of your intellect, the experiences you've garnered help propel you forward like a comet, grow into a planet, and soon become a new universe. This literally means that before long you are the tender and keeper of many fields.

Now is the time for you to build a team that enables you to better juggle the responsibilities and the opportunities that are waiting for you. What I want you to get from this chapter is how to touch everything you have, all the diverse areas of your life, from a position of maximized instinct.

CHAPTER 19

✦

Instincts Adapt

Even when following our instincts, we may unknowingly fall into detrimental patterns. We do it because
at one time a procedure or method worked, but now we
can't seem to notice that what once sufficed no longer sat-
isfies. We know the world is constantly changing around
us, but we remain several paces behind our instincts'
attempt to keep up with those changes. Adjusting to new
worlds, new ideas, and new concepts is important in any
sphere of life, but perhaps even more when you're living
by instinct.

All past practices aren't always good practices.
Please understand this isn't a clarion call to change for
the sake of changing. No, it is more aptly a challenge
to remain vigilant to changes around you and to make
adjustments to old ideas and concepts that may have
outlived their usefulness. In a relationship, matrimony

slides into monotony. In a job, enthusiasm melts into mediocrity. In a company, irreplaceable becomes irrelevant. In a ministry, determination deteriorates into decoration. No matter your perspective or preference, old ideas that are unchallenged become the gateway to antiquation.

I'm often forced to wrestle my own attraction to the familiar. My need to have consistency often has to be overhauled to sustain the adventure of achieving traditional outcomes in nonconventional ways. My desired objectives may not have changed, but my methods constantly have to adapt to keep pace with an ever-changing world. Because, like it or not, the ground moves under our feet whether we feel it or not. If you want to remain in the room with the chosen and not in the basement of relics, then your ideas must remain fluid and your approach flexible as you implement those ideas.

Some years ago, we kept in contact with our partners by mailing them letters. It was important and necessary, effective and engaging. I got most of my responses from mail, and we had companies to assist us with mailing from our database. Now, the contracts with those companies remained in place, but busyness kept me from noticing that we were doing the same things we had always done with increasingly fewer results. We were mailing people who were *e-mailing* us back. Duh! It seems obvious that a change was necessary, doesn't it?

Well, it would if I weren't lulled to sleep by busyness and distraction. I suppose it took almost a year for Rip Van Winkle here to wake up and smell the coffee. The world had changed right under my feet, but my system of reaching people had not changed to keep up. Once I recognized the problem, I had to readjust systems and discovered that the old company helping us mail our audience was snoring in the bed right beside me! They hadn't updated their equipment or method of reaching people to accommodate the new trends, either.

It reminds me of the way my wife continued cooking meals for the kids who used to live with us, and then discovering the abundance of leftovers! Our house was a collection of Tupperware dishes and aluminum foil, all based around the fact that past practices hadn't been challenged while our household had changed. As empty nesters, the garbage disposal started eating up our spoiled leftovers faster than the timer on a microwave can beep!

Once we recognized that our family household had changed, then we began changing our practices to catch up. In all areas we had to have a talk. Maybe we don't need family packs of pork chops when it's just the two of us for dinner. Maybe buying staples such as sugar, flour, and salt in bulk quantities was no longer cost-efficient. We discovered that not being flexible is expensive and more times than not ineffective.

Suddenly I realized that we were caught with our eyes closed to the fact that change anywhere means change everywhere! Less laundry, less utilities, no more leaving the key outside in the planter for late-returning teenagers! We had been recalibrated by the decisions of others and hadn't assessed the impact that their decisions would make on our lives. Change, of course, isn't a bad thing; it's great to see our children become adults and launch their own lives independently. However, if we hadn't adjusted, then we would have continued missing out on some of the benefits of this blessing!

Instinctive Longevity

Our very survival and ability to sustain our success relies on our instincts. For example, an archeological team decided to do research on the remains of the prehistoric bones of the apatosaurus. This was one of the tallest dinosaurs that could get on its hind legs to eat vegetation from the highest foliage of the times. Its past practices had sustained it for years. But as it continued to breed more and more of its species, the growth of the vegetation of its era didn't keep up with the demand. At the saturation point, there were a lot more apatosauruses than treetop foliage! Supply could not keep up with demand.

This creature apparently could not adapt. You need to be sensitive to changes in the environment so you can adapt accordingly.

While other prehistoric animals faced extinction because of predators and climatic changes, the apatosaurus, also known as the brontosaurus, is theorized to have self-destructed simply because it didn't instinctively adapt to the need to bend its neck and eat from the foliage a little lower on the trees. The entire species could've likely lasted longer had the apatosauruses not been inflexible in their ability to move beyond their past practice. The much-needed food source was literally a short radius from where they faced total depletion. Just below barren branches grew an abundant food source that would have easily nourished them.

This illustration takes the term *stiff-necked* to a new level! When you or those who assist you develop a stiff-necked view of the possibilities around you, it can have lethal consequences. Increase the radius of your thinking and creativity, and you will find new foliage. We see it every day in second marriages, new managements in old business, and new leadership in churches. We see it in changing the staff at a school. It's a tragedy when someone with less rigidity can turn your wilderness into a vegetable garden by implementing simple things that were within your view but off your radar because of your commitment to "the way we do things."

Think about it this way: if you are too predictable in any area of your life, you may be paving the way to your own extinction! Reflect for a moment on how you usually recognize and regard the changes around you. Is your inability to adapt to the world around you your greatest enemy? Could it be possible that you could meet traditional needs in contemporary ways?

The real challenge for many people, marriages, ministries, and companies is that they don't have people around them with enough neck-stretching enthusiasm to mix up their sources of inspiration and innovation. The tops of their trees become stripped of the creative nourishment that's required to adapt and to thrive! They need people who are always seeing changing trends, birthing new ideas, and glimpsing new horizons. They need nimble minds and maybe agile necks to bend the conventional rules and go against the grain when necessary.

Unorthodox thinkers are creative. They deviate from the traditional to the transformative and break into new foliage by discerning the times and making the changes necessary to at least keep things the same if not make them better! Stiff-necked people will destroy vital opportunities because they can't adapt to trends and changes around them—they remain too intent on defining themselves by past practices. They think "I have never" when they really mean "I can't evolve." Sadly, they often end up in the valley of dry bones.

Better Instincts, Best Practices

As you instinctively adapt your past practices to the changes around you, please understand that your adjustments may or may not be the best practices. Past practices never take the place of best practices. And best practices are often modified by changing seasons and stages of evolving. What is best when you are twenty may not be best when you are fifty. What is best when you are single may not be best when you are married.

Understand that even if you're not running a company, you still have a brand. Your personal brand may keep its core values, but it's dangerous to hold on to antiquated practices. Best practices are always affected by new inventions, new relationships, and new opportunities. People who are afraid of change are afraid of success.

In my ministry I've learned that my core values seldom need adjustment. These are the ethical ideologies that define who we are as a church. But at the same time, if I do everything the way I did when I started out, I'm not really growing at all. The message doesn't change, but the method must always evolve.

In my private business, the same principle applies in even greater ways. Not only does the method change, but sometimes the message changes also. Depending on new experiences that alter how we do business, and new opportunities that unleash possibilities that weren't originally an option, we have to adapt.

So periodically I've learned to do assessments of what was and what is. In my marriage from time to time my wife and I will go on more frequent dates.

During these seasons, we explore each other's lives again and discuss who we've become. As a result, we've learned that one of the most lethal toxins to our relationship is predictability. Keeping our life together fresh means not taking each other for granted and assuming what used to bring each other joy is still the same. So as we age and evolve what really helps is open-mindedness. Giving each other the right to grow and change together helps us not to grow apart.

Relearning what you thought you knew well is important in every facet of life. It is presumptuous to think that silence means contentment. In every area of your life, it's unwise to think that silence is equal to consent. Many times frustration wears silence for the benefit of political correctness. People go with the flow to keep the waters calm. So when you implement changes to keep up with life's unexpected twists and turns, understand that you may encounter some white-water rapids. In other words, giving people the freedom to be honest may cause painful discussions in the short run. But in the long run, it will save you the painful extinction of the vibrancy that makes people want to be around you or work for you.

Anytime you assess someone by who they were without considering who they have become, you are setting yourself up for failure. People change. They evolve. They grow and develop and want to be used at their highest capacity. Stability and security are important, but not at the expense of vibrancy and volatility.

I don't know about you, but I really hate to hear someone say, "I knew you when...," as if this means that it's wrong for me to change. Everything matures— anything that doesn't change is fruit dying on the vine! People are happiest when they can be appreciated for who they are and not just for who they were when you first met them! Our ability to grow and change, to learn and expand, keeps us curious, charismatic, exciting, and fresh!

Like so many aspects of life, this ability to adapt and grow requires you to be instinctive and not just informational. Information is based on past assessments, but instincts signal that something has changed. To be sure, people often transform right in front of us, but we miss it because we're relying on old information or an assessment stuck on our first impression of them.

However, it's as useless as last year's newspaper to rely on what you used to know about a person. People need to be appreciated at the level they are on now. This is especially true when they are constantly improving themselves but imprisoned by how your limited view contains them. In order to be sensitive to those changes, you have to pay attention to people. Looking at a person is far different from just seeing them. Such alertness can stop you from longing for something that is really accessible to you but not detected by you! I've been there.

Right Under Your Nose

A few years ago I was interviewing candidates for a very important position in my organization. I had hired a firm to assist me, as I had come to learn that intellectual capital is very important in business. In many ways smart people are more significant to growth than economic capital. This position would likely transform my company and allow me to delegate responsibilities that should rightfully be done by someone else. I had huge respect for the position, and I had headhunters searching high and low for a person who could grasp quickly the culture in our business and move dexterously into innovation with little disruption to the chemistry that defined us.

I reviewed some wonderful résumés—of course, résumés are *always* wonderful! But as we began to vet them, I found that most of the applicants weren't suitable for the position I was trying desperately to fill. I became frustrated that it was so challenging to find the right person.

As the search continued, one day I was riding to an appointment with an employee relatively new to our company. He said, "You know, I think Mr. Wilson"—not his real name—"would be tremendous for that role!" Maintaining a poker face, I thought to myself, "That's ridiculous."

I had known Mr. Wilson for years, and what he did

for us was nowhere near what this new position called for. But I have a habit of playing most conversations over a time or two before filing them away. And the more I thought about it, the more this conversation refused to be deleted. In fact, the more I thought about how much Mr. Wilson had grown as a person and enhanced himself along the way, the more I thought my new hire was right. So I ended up hiring Mr. Wilson into that role, and he has been a huge asset ever since.

At the time, however, I was puzzled. How could someone with no real background in this particular area come into my organization and see things that I, as its founder, couldn't even see? I finally realized that my past defining of Mr. Wilson had blinded me to future potentials. It was amazing to me that what I was searching for was right under my nose and I was not seeing it. Clearly, I almost overlooked the fact that some of my greatest resources were already with me. Yet I had misfiled them because I had seen them as they were and not as they had become.

My friend, take a good look at your life. Take a close inspection of those you have around you. You may be crying out for something or someone that is closer to you than you would've ever imagined. My challenge to you is to lower your neck, increase your scope, and never assume that what you saw before is all that there is to see! Reexamine what you have and who is near you. Don't be afraid to let others see how you have instinctively changed!

CHAPTER 20

<figure>❧</figure>

Treetop Instincts

Some time ago I was asked to be a guest journalist and contribute a series of op-eds for a prestigious media outlet. Despite my fears that my writing style and mental prowess could not compare with the impressive list of other contributors participating in the forum, I seized the opportunity and began to chronicle ideas. For my topic I chose a fairly interesting but not controversial subject and addressed it with all the research and writing skill I could muster.

This was indeed a new forum for me, and like most of us, whenever I step into a new arena, I want to do my very best work. So before submitting my entry, I passed it around to a few of my brightest colleagues who all pronounced it a stellar presentation worthy of the brand of that notable forum. Then with a sense of confidence I hit the Send button, and a few milliseconds later, it was in the hands of the editor. She oohed and awed about it in her response, and we started a process I really enjoyed...until I read the printed copy!

Immediately upon publication, the online comments poured in and everyone had something to say. Some were contributing ideas and thoughts, others were complimentary and encouraging. But then I came to the rants and insults, and my heart sank into my shoes. I read post after post filled with such astonishingly acrimonious remarks.

Some of my negative responders attacked me as an individual, even though they actually don't know me and what I'm all about. Other critics attacked the topic of my article. A few didn't even seem related to what I had written—they just wanted to vent.

Needless to say, I was just floored. Shocked and appalled, yet still determined to penetrate the standards and earn their readers' respect, I wrote another article for the forum. The results were the same.

By the time I reached deadline for my fourth contribution, I made some excuse for not contributing to the next edition and prepared to retire from the forum, assuming I was out of my league and over my head. However, a few weeks later I ran into the editor at a conference. She immediately asked, "Why have you stopped contributing to our forum?"

Shamefully, I said, "I got the impression I really didn't measure up to the standards of your readers."

"You're kidding!" she exclaimed in shock. "Why, your entries were some of our highest-rated ones!"

Now I was the one shocked. So I began to explain to her about the consistently negative comments I had encountered after each article. She actually laughed right in my face and said, "Those people aren't our audience! Our demographic is largely intellectuals who read for content and seldom comment other than to express another philosophical idea they deem significant enough to add to the dialog. I seldom even read the comments after the article! Those shrill, angry voices don't want to be understood. They just want to make noise. They have nothing of substance to say!"

I laughed and walked away, disappointed with myself for allowing a few minor-league curveballs to knock me out of a major league opportunity. Why did I allow "little" to remove me from "much"?

For quite some time, I couldn't explain why my sensitivity had assaulted my opportunity. It wasn't like me to be so easily intimidated.

But then I saw the giraffes.

Taste the Treetops

My defensive reaction remained a mystery until it came to mind during my safari. Watching a herd of giraffes illustrate a fundamentally instinctive principle, I found my answer from this surprising group of nature's towering tutors. Outside Johannesburg, across the South African plain, a galloping group of giraffes instructed me on what it means to eat at eye level.

From my guide, along with some online research, I learned giraffes are even-toed ungulates, the tallest mammals on earth. The males can reach heights of twenty feet in the air, craning their six- to seven-foot necks above their torsos. A stately species indeed, with their elongated necks, lithe bodies, and strong legs, they move graciously and gingerly with an almost regal bearing. They struck me as the NBA team of the zoological kingdom, only with the movements of a ballerina as well as a basketball player.

I watched the giraffes stroll onto the plains like a float in a Thanksgiving Day parade, and it wasn't until they stopped to have an outdoor lunch that they taught me their powerful lesson. In spite of their long necks, which would allow them the ability to lower their heads to almost ground level, they didn't drop their heads but always ate from the tops of the trees. I was mesmerized.

I had never really considered how giraffes eat, assuming they grazed like other animals. But watching them stretch and munch mouthfuls of leafy green entrees, I was struck by their own unique, up-in-the-air style. They clearly did not graze from the ground like many of the other creatures around their ankles. They liked the treetops.

And that's when I realized what I had done wrong in the situation with my forum. The small herd of magnificent mammals—their group is often called a "tower," fittingly enough—might as well have used a chalkboard to teach me their truth. Like the giraffe, I had aspired to new heights, but I couldn't keep my gaze at eye level because of the clamor around my feet. I had walked away from a twenty-foot opportunity because of the chatter I heard from two-foot thinkers!

I failed to realize that once you reach a certain level, you can't be offended by other species who continue looking up from the ground! Once you get to a certain stature, you can't find nourishment in low places. Just because turtles dwell at your feet doesn't mean you should come down from your height and barter with, debate, or eat alongside them. As you rise, you must adjust your source of nourishment and affirmation accordingly. Yes, like the dinosaurs, there are times when you must adapt and bend your neck to eat—but only if there's no nourishment from the top!

When your influence and intellect evolve, you can't move forward without someone behind you criticizing your every move. Instead of eating a huge gourmet meal of the mud they're slinging, I learned to raise my eating habits to my sight line. I learned to always get a table on the top floor of thought and use a barometer commensurate with my own vision and goals to measure my efforts.

Feeding from the Front

How fitting that this giant of an animal eats from the tops of the trees, since that's what he sees. However, his turtle friends' sights are too low for a meaningful dialog with those twenty feet above them. Whenever you collide with people whose sight lines are limited by the view they have of the world, it's a futile exercise to expect them to see what you see.

And if they can't see it, they certainly can't partake of the wisdom your height allows you to have. If you're sitting in a rooftop restaurant, you can't have a conversation with someone sitting at a sidewalk café! My status had moved, but my appetite for acceptance was still down at the level of the turtles. This incident resulted in my forfeiting a treetop moment.

And I know I'm not the only one. It's been amazing to notice how many people think like giraffes but eat like turtles. As a young twenty-something preacher, I encountered an older man from my church who asked what I thought he should do about his painful marriage. Truth be told, the complications of his relationship with his wife were far beyond my experience at the time. So after listening to him describe their issues with communication, trust, and jealousy, I hastily replied, "Divorce her."

Now before you judge me for my mistake, please realize that my young mind wasn't experienced with the hardships inherent in keeping a family afloat. My children were small, my wife was young, and my pastoral counseling experience limited. Needless to say, the man who sought my advice found it terribly adolescent. He was polite, but I could see the disappointment in his eyes.

No matter how much I cared about him and wanted to help, sometimes love isn't enough to span the gap between the hypothetical and the holistic, the evolutionary and the revolutionary. We were living in two different worlds, we were planets in different orbits, and my counsel was limited by the space between us. He turned to me for wisdom, but I could not reach the point from which he was asking. As you can see, in this case I was the turtle and he was the giraffe. My limited perspectives informed my worldview. I hadn't lived long enough to give a balanced view of what he should do.

Most of our opinions are based upon perspective. While you must respect everyone's right to offer an opinion, you cannot walk in the wisdom of someone who has never lived on your level. In short, a turtle and a giraffe can occupy the same space, but they will never have the same sights! You can't wreck your neck to graze the grass, and he can't touch the treetops. Stay clear of his complaints and counsel. He is only reacting to his perspective.

Anyone who has lived very long shudders today at the ideas they had twenty years ago. Perspectives mature and ideas change as time and experiences allow you to find that what you thought in the grass seems ridiculous in the trees. That's why it's unwise to shout from the rooftop—or the laptop—messages that you may not believe tomorrow.

It's remarkable that giraffes aren't born with long necks. If they were, then birth would be like trying to shove a bazooka through a keyhole! God, in his infinite wisdom, develops the giraffe's neck once it's outside the womb. Similarly, our necks grow with time and extend our views with experiences and opportunities that forever alter our perspectives. The same plot we saw from the ground looks a lot different from the air!

I also discovered that giraffes generally don't travel in herds. They gather in groups from time to time, but overall their survival skills don't depend on their peers. Now, most people enjoy it when public consensus aligns with their decisions. But we must not hinder our progress by requiring others' approval for the decisions that we alone must make.

This principle exceeds socialization and protrudes into what you read and need for intellectual stimulation. Because we are so impressionable as a species, you soon take on the attributes of the group you gallop with, and it will influence the outcome and the destination. I'm not sure why giraffes don't have the herding instinct we see in so many other species, but I appreciate the reminder. The busier we become in life, the more we must make sure the quality—not the quantity—of our relationships counts. The demands we face don't allow for casual, meaningless socialization.

Fight or Flight

With my new insight, I made a mental note to study giraffes more closely for other clues that would sustain my stature and steady my process of survival in new arenas. They had much to teach me. I learned that a male giraffe uses his neck as a weapon. I learned that when mating season comes, the male competes for the female by fighting off other contenders with the sheer force and size of his neck. He wields it like a sword, often dismantling his opponent's aspirations with the sheer force of his muscled mane. This is nature's way of maintaining only the strongest of future genera-tions of giraffes.

You see, height always means leverage. The height of your connections, the height of your influence, the height of your ideas and creativity, they all converge to elevate you to an airspace where others can't com-pete. So as you escalate in status, understand that your ability to ascend is a weapon unto itself. Your height remains an advantage until you come out of your class and start battling with a turtle.

Now, I know it may be tempting, especially because you may assume you are more powerful or talented than your opponents—and maybe you are. But when you stoop to ground level to battle your belittlers, you could lose your leverage and land on your back! Leaders who have reached a new height don't stoop down to prove a point or ward off an assault. They know that even if you win, it doesn't compare with what you lose when you fight beneath yourself.

The giraffe seldom bends low. Even when he drinks, which is infrequently, he retains the water for long periods of time. As fully loaded as a new Mercedes 500 SEL, a giraffe's neck contains a highly complex vascular system that keeps him from blacking out when he lowers his head into the radius of the water he drinks. He can bend it and drink; but he is not designed to spend long lengths of time with his head down. Consequently, he seldom drinks, and like his cousin the camel, he retains what he does drink for long periods of time.

Instinctive leaders and the innovative thinkers understand that to "keep their head up" may mean more than just staying encouraged. It could be a dire warning against acquiescing to the tactics of the terrorist who seeks their demise. What others are saying often isn't as dangerous as it could be until you lower your head to respond! Maintain your current level of vision, and don't droop to the petty politics percolating below. It would be tragic for you to lose your balance and fall from your height responding to the hecklers who only envy your position.

If those who follow your lead see you drop your head long enough, they may eventually question your strength as a leader. Sure, they may encourage you to enter a fight at first, but eventually they realize that your energies are wasted on ground-level concerns while the larger agenda floats above you. They lose confidence in you.

The height to which your giftedness may carry you may mean leaving the lower greenery to the folks whose mouths and eyes line up to that terrain beneath you.

Feed What's Feeding You

Standing there beside the Jeep in South Africa, I kept my gaze focused on my new fascination, aware of what I was about to discover: giraffes were much more complicated than they appeared. It wasn't until my guide, a zoologist, began telling me about them that I realized how much I didn't know.

For instance, no one can deny the majestic beauty of the giraffe with its various shades of brown, a divine mosaic of chocolates and caramels painted by God himself. But as beautiful as the external view may be, the logistical diagram of its inner construction is where the mind staggers in sheer awe.

Its beautiful curvaceous hide is a work of art when it moves. Beneath its artistic exterior is a richly well-thought-out biological masterpiece. The giraffe holds within its chest the largest heart of its species, a twenty-five-pound muscular pump capable of sending blood all the way up its massive neck to its head and brain.

Somehow the giraffe, by feeding from the tops of trees, nourishes this extraordinary heart. In its simplest form, the circulatory system forms a circle by which the body feeds itself.

You must always remember to feed what's feeding you; this cycle of nourishment is the source of our very survival. If it's a marriage, you have to feed it. If it's a business, you must pour resources back into it. If it's a church, a club, a friendship, an educational institution—whatever it is that stimulates you, gives you energy, and helps you be your best self—you must feed it in turn.

The heart of the car is the engine. It doesn't matter how the wheels glisten or how sophisticated is the computer technology that operates its systems. If there is no engine, nothing else is energized. The heart of the corporation is human resources. This is the department that hires and supports the right staff to fuel the vision of the CEO. If you don't build up your human resources, the company will eventually go code blue. You'll learn the hard way that talented, committed people really are your greatest resources.

The heart of the church is the Gospel. If the building is loaded with stained glass, great music, and social services but loses its core message of salvation, then it may be a great organization but it certainly isn't a church. For the brain to be sustained, the heart must produce a steady flow of lifeblood. The two must work together to move the body in synchronicity, or you will never reach the heights for which you were created.

So ask yourself, what feeds your dream?

Heads and Hearts

At the heart of our instincts, we discover our primary purpose. Our purpose provides the message or mission by which we live out our gifts and talents. Our instinctive life mission cannot be purposeless and powerful. In film development, the heart of the movie is the script. If the screenplay doesn't feed the actor the lines she needs to develop a compelling character, then even the greatest actor becomes powerless to deliver the punch.

Have you ever seen someone have a heart attack? Their eyes go dim, their pulse stops, their mouth goes dry, and their pupils dilate. Why such reactions in the head when it's the heart that's malfunctioning? Obviously, the head along with the rest of the body manifests the effects of the heart shutting down. It is from the heart that the head and body have life.

The giraffe has a tongue like no other animal. It can reach around branches and pull down fruit, and its fur-covered horns are strong enough to ram through any obstacle in its path. However, none of its attributes and strengths matter without the heart energizing the activity. Yes, the heart must function properly to sustain the body.

When I teach leadership courses, I compare the relationship between leaders and those they lead to a traveler moving through the desert on a camel with only one canteen of water. If the camel drinks all the water, it survives and the passenger dies. But if the passenger drinks all the water and the camel dies, then the passenger dies of sunstroke!

Life sometimes presents us with strange teachers, but their lessons are often the most memorable. This has certainly been my experience with sighting a group of giraffes in the African bush. They immediately triggered an epiphany that allowed me to realize why I had let my loudest critics demotivate my budding journalistic efforts.

But more important, the giraffe inspired me to want to reach higher, extend my abilities farther, and taste new treetops. If you want to live by instinct, feed your heart and stretch to the treetops!

CHAPTER 21

✦

All That Is Within You

I can still remember my friend the zoologist sharing with me how even the angles of certain animals' teeth were designed to gnaw at branches as a source of pruning so that both the food chain and cycle of life would not be broken. I thought to myself, "Look at how God has made all needs to coincide so that the animal's hunger serves as a gardening tool for the branches that provide his food!" Relentless reliance on instinct not only supplies what we need but also becomes the vehicle by which all else around us is affected and sustained.

As we conclude, I hope your confidence is greater, your aim sharper, and your awareness of your innate abilities more finely honed. More fully immersed in the wellspring of your instincts, you will have an increased impact on the target before you. Whether you're aiming at a change in career or just hoping to parent a child, I believe the answers we often seek from those around us are actually buried somewhere within us.

"As thy days are, so shall thy strength be" literally means that in proportion to the demand, the resource emerges to fulfill the need. You have what you need when you need it! Maybe not always exactly when you *want* it—but when you *need* it.

Primal But Not Primitive

Once again, I want to be sure you understand that these concepts are not meant to give you any formula or template for success but to awaken what may be dormant or underutilized in your life. Sometimes recognizing the resources already available to us can be the most empowering moment of all. We are most effective when we draw from every God-given resource we have been given to survive in this world. Now with the full armor of all that has been given to you, it's time to change the dynamics of the game.

We've had an exciting journey through concepts and precepts, jungles and junctures, as we've explored the various nuances to developing a more effective life by using our instincts. However, all of it means nothing if we do not recognize that the investment of ideas merely prepares us for the opportunities with which we've been graced in our individual lives. If you believe as I do that we have been divinely prewired for a master purpose beyond ourselves, you then should be equally excited to realize that tapping into your instincts acknowledges your own unique purpose on this earth.

You see, our instincts not only exist to enhance our experience here on earth; they also provide evidence of a mastermind above us who placed all that we would need within us. I believe that what God has given us is his gift to us. How we utilize what we've been given is our gift back to him. By shedding fresh light on something profoundly primal but not primitive within us, I've challenged you to consider new paradigms and empowered you to shatter the limitations of fear and frustration blocking your liberation.

Much of our attention has been invested into the introspective examination of bundling all that is within us to affect all that is around us. We now clearly understand that intellect without instinct is like a head without a heart. When we embrace all that is intellectual and psychological without including the deeply spiritual, the instinctive inclinations of our hearts limit us unnecessarily. Remember, Scripture tells us that out of the *heart* flows the issues of life—not out of the head!

You Have What It Takes

Recognize the adequacy of what is within you to survive and succeed amid all you face. You do have what it takes to master the outward challenges as you release your inner resources. But if you're going to accomplish this awakening of instinct within you, it's time to act. You must connect ideas to ideals and excitement to action. You must do more with this book than place it on a shelf or file it away in your electronic reading device.

Don't get me wrong. I love being able to share my ideas here with you in these pages. Reading is the gymnasium of the mind. It is the place where thoughts are exercised and minds are stretched and challenged. However, through tranquility and deep reflection we are able to search the heart for answers that the mind alone doesn't contain. The mind may guide you in what to do, but the heart affirms your passion to do it. This is what will ultimately move you to motion.

Somewhere in your passions lie the clues to your deeper purpose. It is my hope that you will recognize the divine investment placed within you and garner all your resources to steward this treasure for the future before you. In short, you have what it takes! All that you need is within you and can be accessed instinctively. Understanding this truth secretes confidence, which I'm convinced has a lot to do with overcoming obstacles and releasing your inherent, resilient power.

It is an exciting moment in history to have the privilege to see innovation spring forward so quickly and technology create so many forums through which we can convey our ideas. And yet, while we have more ways to exchange ideas as a result of that technological influence, none of the iPads, iPhones, Skypes, Google chats, and Facebook exchanges can create the thoughts we want to exchange. They are designed only to enhance the way we convey them.

Absolutely nothing we have created will replace how we have been created. These technological artifacts assist us in communicating ideas, but none of them create the ideas we communicate. The data they transfer, share, and compute is only what we program in them. So then the most precious resource we have to date is not around us but *inside* of us.

The demands of the times and the pace of communication has heightened to the degree that we can dialog with others all over the world in real time without physically leaving our living room couch. But this global connectivity isn't what makes us a great society. What makes us great is not the vehicles from which we speak, but rather that which we have to say through them.

So what is your deepest, truest message that you want to convey to the world? This is the moment that we need to clear our minds from the clutter and allow our instincts to guide the process of creative reasoning. If we can strengthen what is within us, we can change that which is around us. I am excited to know that we are only one domino-toppling thought away from a cure for HIV-AIDS. I am excited that we are gaining ground on dread diseases like cancer, heart disease, Alzheimer's, and autism. Even at this very moment, the solutions to world poverty and global warming are locked in someone's mind and about to be unleashed by their instincts. Whoever holds the key to changing the world can't be someone who runs with the herd and fits in with the pack. Our world has always advanced through trailblazers who broke boundaries and shattered limitations.

Now I must confess, it is unlikely that any of these tasks are likely to be vanquished by someone like me. But that's okay. I will be happy to tackle the challenges within my view even if they gain no notoriety in the world of medicine nor instigate world peace. If my instincts do not lead me to a more perfect world, and only succeed in granting me a more peaceful home, I will still be fulfilled.

If my instincts can aid me in my affairs and can be used to settle the level of problems my life unfolds, then I am still content. At the end of the day, I realize that all great people will not be famous. And all famous people will not be great. Instinct was never meant to ensure our recognition. Instinct may remain incognito but always inspires and initiates your success.

It propels us forward—and we need not all travel at the same speed. As we've seen, one of the gifts of our instinct is timing and knowing the pace of our current season. As long as we're moving forward, we will reach our destination.

It is so comforting to remember that we're equipped by what's within us to respond to the demands of what's around us at any given time. It may not feel like we're in sync with those pressures around us, but I'm convinced that's often because we're not following the tempo within.

Ready, Aim, Pull

I often think of those affluent men who practice their sporting reflexes by enjoying the challenge of skeet shooting. Clad in the dapper hunting fashion of the sport, these shooters have oiled their guns and packed a rucksack, and then head into the wild to practice their aim. Their competition is fierce, either against one another or their own abilities, as they take their loaded shotguns and move them into a position of anticipatory release. Obviously confident that his gun is loaded and the barrel clean, each marksman gingerly rests the butt of his gun against his shoulder, providing stability but also the flexibility necessary to avoid the full brunt of recoil. Then, and only then, does he shout, "Pull!"

Faster than a lightning bolt flashing across the sky, the designated operator then releases the automated device propelling the small clay disc, or skeet, into the air hundreds of feet above the shooter. The gunman aligns his vision, using his knowledge of the disc's expected trajectory, the physical reflexes of his arm, and, most important, his trigger finger to fire his shot at the inanimate target. If he is successful, a spray of clay shards soon falls to the ground around his feet.

Though I have never done it myself, I've observed the sport enough to know that the shooter has only a brief few seconds to align what he has on the ground with what is being catapulted into the air. While I only shot pictures of the beautiful creatures we encountered on safari, I still know the importance of an acute sense of timing. The right shot at the wrong time becomes just as impotent as a poor shot.

This same sensitivity to timing has guided my life. It is reflected in the famous line from the Lord's Prayer, "Give us this day our daily bread." In other words, Lord, please don't wait until tomorrow to give me what I need today!

Similarly, we ourselves are reminded to use what we've already been given this day, the resources within us that can provide sustenance for life's journey. Let me be found possessing what I need at the pace of the challenges I face. We must trust our instincts to release the instructions we need commensurate with the stage and age where we find ourselves.

Nothing hovers around you that you cannot overcome by leveraging what you already know as well as your instincts, that which you know but don't realize you know. Right now, today, even as you read these very words—this is the moment to align what you've learned with what is deep inside you. This is the time to look ahead and reconsider the obstacles that block your sight line of future success.

By now, I hope you've reconsidered your view of these barriers. Most obstructions are merely opportunities in masquerade. You no longer need to adhere to the conditions of a cage you have left behind. Especially when they will cause you to fall prey to larger predators within the new jungles you're facing. To survive as well as thrive, you must activate your instincts in sync with the life you lead.

Like the gunman who moves his rifle in rhythm with his target—or in my case, the photographer on safari snapping a mighty elephant's pic, you must squeeze without missing the right moment. You now have the fluidity of thought to break rhythm with normalcy and aim at destiny with a heightened awareness of your instinctive prewiring, a gift imbued within us by God himself.

It is my prayer that none of us will allow where we start to determine how we finish. It is my hope that ultimately we would garner the fortitude and tenacity to plunge beyond the boundaries of the obvious and into the opportunities our life affords us. In this brief shining moment, you and I must activate all that is within us to initiate the instinctive process and planning inherent to the greater purpose of the One who created us.

The design is not greater than the designer, so ultimately we acknowledge his handiwork in all that he has placed within us. Understanding how wonderfully and thoughtfully we were brought into existence, our best and most instinctive response is simply to live according to this abundance we've been given. It is our way of saying yes to what was in God's mind when we were formed. It is our way of letting our Creator know we're ready for the next opportunity.

As you prepare to release all the aim, energy, and intellect now loaded into your instincts, there's only one thing left to say as you squeeze the trigger.

"Pull!"

Acknowledgments

Just as our instincts provide the rhythm for our life's melody, they also help us discover others moving to the same beat. People from the same tribe of tempo as my own have allowed me to expand and enhance my message the way an orchestra transforms notes on the page. I'm grateful to each and every one of them for their contributions, instinctive and otherwise, to this book.

I'm delighted to begin a new publishing partnership with my friends at Hachette. Rolf Zettersten and his team at FaithWords embraced the message of *Instinct* from the beginning and shared a vision bigger than either of us could have imagined alone. Thank you, Rolf, and the entire Hachette team who worked on this book.

The editorial insight of Adrienne Ingrum also made this a better book. I also appreciate the assistance of Lauren Rohrig and Mark Steven Long.

I would like to thank Dr. Jill Waggoner-Jones for her medical insight into the fascinating world of cell development in the human body. Kelly R. Sedgwick and Regina Lewis helped immeasurably with their willingness to research and provide supporting data to validate my ideas.

I'm indebted to my team at TDJ Enterprises, especially Zunoraine Holmes for his many contributions and coordinations that have kept *Instinct* and all its pieces working together harmoniously. You always keep up with the beat no matter how fast or loud it becomes. Thanks, Z!

Dudley Delffs provided his instinctive wisdom on writing and editorial expertise to the process of building this book. We share a love for language, and I'm so grateful for his ongoing commitment to me and my message.

I cannot say enough good things about Jan Miller and Shannon Marven and their team at Dupree/ Miller & Associates. They know the value of being guided by instincts, and I'm so glad we move to the same rhythm! Their tireless efforts on my behalf speak louder than words about their passionate investment in all my endeavors, and I'm forever indebted to them.

No one can be led by their instincts without encouragement, support, and influence from their family. My children have taught me more than they realize about what it means to discover the uniqueness within each of us. Thank you, Jermaine, Jamar, Cora, Sarah, and Dexter for the privilege of seeing you follow your own instincts successfully into adulthood. My wonderful wife, Serita, is a woman who lives by her instinctive ability to bring grace, beauty, and peace wherever she goes. She has always encouraged me to follow my instincts, and I have learned so much by witnessing the way her instincts operate. My love and thanks to you all!

About the Author

T.D. Jakes, CEO of TDJ Enterprises

T.D. Jakes is a master communicator, philanthropist, and multidimensional business leader. As CEO of TDJ Enterprises, he has more than 30 books in print; to date his films have grossed nearly $100 million at the box office; and he has an international speaking platform that has galvanized crowds of 800,000. As a thought leader he has commanded stages from the Aspen Institute to SMU to the Peter Drucker CEO Forum. As CEO and founder of the T.D. Jakes School of Leadership, he provides career development tools to business leaders.

He is the founder and pastor of The Potter's House of Dallas, Inc. On Sundays he is pastor to more than 30,000, with millions of worldwide followers online via Facebook, Twitter, and Instagram. He lives in Dallas with his wife and five children. Visit www.tdjakes.com.

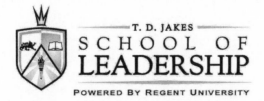